Leadership in Administration

A Sociological Interpretation

Leadership in Administration

A Sociological Interpretation

PHILIP SELZNICK

University of California, Berkeley

University of California Press
Berkeley, Los Angeles, London

To Gertrude

University of California Press
Berkeley and Los Angeles, California
University of California Press, Ltd.
London, England

Copyright © 1957 by Harper & Row, Publishers, Incorporated
California Paperback Edition 1984

ISBN: 978-0-520-04994-9

Library of Congress Catalog Card Number 57-11350

Printed in the United States of America

12 11 10 09

14 13 12 11 10

Preface to
the California Edition

Leadership in Administration was published in 1957. In response to a modest but steady demand it has remained in print ever since. I am pleased that the University of California Press has undertaken to publish this paperbound edition. The original text is reprinted here without alteration.

This essay began as an attempt to clarify a perspective I had brought to bear in two previous books, *TVA and the Grass Roots* (1949) and *The Organizational Weapon* (1952). These very different subjects—one an innovative government agency, the other a political instrument of Marxist-Leninist ideology—were studied as examples of organizational development and character-formation. I was persuaded that the principles I was developing, which were based on sociological theory, could aid in the diagnosis of a wide variety of organizations. After some further research, especially on military and business organization, I ventured to state those principles. I thought it would be helpful to do so within the framework of a theory of leadership.

I did not intend this to be more than a tentative formulation, but I was drawn to other (through related) studies of law and society,[1] and have not returned to the specific ideas developed here. In the meantime my views became known in some quarters as the "institutional" perspective in organization theory.[2] Indeed, as the reader of this essay will quickly discover, how organizations become institutions, and what problems and opportunities are thus created, is a central theme of the work.

The institutional approach has a practical relevance, above all because it is a voice of resistance to the culture of shortsightedness. In recent years we have come to understand that the American penchant for quick returns has undermined our prosperity and weakened our institutions. When business leaders indulge in unproductive conglomeration, or tie the rewards of highly mobile executives to last quarter's bottom line, they overemphasize immediate financial gain to the detriment of solid investment. But myopia in business is only part of a shortsightedness that afflicts the whole of American society. Our major institutions—political, legal, educational, industrial—are under pressure to perform in the short run and have little support, from within or without, for a longer view of what they are doing and where they are going.

As I indicated on p. 143, "the long run" refers not to time

---

[1] In *Law, Society, and Industrial Justice* (New York: Russell Sage, 1969) I analyzed the "legal worth" of modern management and human relations (chap. 3), as well as the role of collective bargaining in organizational development. That study is an elaboration of the institutional and political perspective of *Leadership in Administration* but focuses more sharply on "governance" as a vital aspect of effective management.

[2] See Charles Perrow, *Complex Organizations: A Critical Essay* (Glenview, Ill.: Scott, Foresman, 1979), chap. 5; W. Richard Scott, *Organizations: Rational, Natural, and Open Systems* (Englewood Cliffs, N.J.: Prentice-Hall, 1981), pp. 90ff. See also Sheldon S. Wolin, *Politics and Vision* (Boston: Little, Brown, 1960), chap. 10, and my rejoinder in Amitai Etzioni (ed.), *A Sociological Reader on Complex Organizations* (New York: Holt, Rinehart, and Winston, 2d. ed., 1969), pp. 149–154.

as such but to the larger consequences of what we do—the outcome for basic competence or for personal or institutional identity. For example, how does modern information technology, which vastly increases the opportunity for quick reactions, affect the competence of an organization to develop and sustain strategic perspectives? We need to learn from experience, and from precise data wherever possible, but what is *relevant* experience can only be determined by bringing to bear a sound understanding of goals and missions, capabilities and limits.

I do not mean to disparage the pragmatic impulse in American life. It is wise to be skeptical of abstractions; it is sensible to ask what difference an idea makes for today's problems and today's satisfactions. But our institutions would be better served if the lessons of that peculiarly American philosophy, the pragmatism of William James and John Dewey, were better understood. In that perspective, practical judgment must always be tied to the here-and-now; it must be rooted in genuine problems; it must be tested by experienced pain and satisfaction. But that is not the end of wisdom. In the philosophy of pragmatism all policy-making, indeed all of life, should reflect informed awareness of what is worth having, doing, and being. Pragmatism is not a flight from principle. It is an argument for discovering principles and for making them relevant to everyday life.

As I write these lines we are in the midst of a heady effort to assess and assimilate the successes of Japanese industry. The Japanese have been highly pragmatic, by any standard, but they have not identified being practical with short-run approaches to investment, employment policy, or quality control. In this they have been sustained by a culture that encourages personal discipline and group solidarity. Americans cannot become Japanese but they can learn that vigorous competition need not presume a fragmented social order; that capitalism can thrive without unbridled economic freedom; and that a spirit of cooperation within organizations must prevail if high levels of productivity and quality are to be achieved.

It may well be that American culture—more unruly, more individualist, more careless of tradition—is not a rich resource for what Chester I. Barnard called "cooperative systems."[3] He was right, of course, that all organization is founded in cooperation. But an enterprise can prosper, under congenial conditions, if it does no more than meet minimal standards of solidarity, communication, and leadership. For Americans the lesson of cooperation has been hard to learn. We have depended for success on other advantages, especially innovative talent and the sheer weight of resources. For a long time, low levels of efficiency could be accepted. That time is past, however, and in the absence of a supportive culture American management will depend more than ever on self-conscious application—and patient testing—of organizational theories.

Philip Selznick

Berkeley, California
June, 1983

[3] *The Functions of the Executive* (Cambridge: Harvard University Press, 1938).

Preface

This essay outlines a perspective for the study of leadership in administrative organizations. It was written in the conviction that more reflective, theoretical discussion is needed to guide the gathering of facts and the diagnosis of troubles. This subject, like the larger study of government and society, requires our profoundest intellectual concern. We shall not find any simple prescriptions for sound organizational leadership; nor will it be purchased with a bag of tricks and gadgets. It requires nothing less than the proper ordering of human affairs, including the establishment of social order, the determination of public interest, and the defense of critical values. Thus conceived, our inquiry has ancient roots. The main problems and issues have been known for a long time, although they need to be restated for the purposes of administrative theory.

This essay was begun while I was associated with The RAND Corporation, and I am deeply grateful to my former colleagues there for providing a creative and challenging intellectual environment. Many others have also been helpful, especially Chester I. Barnard, Herbert Blumer, Leonard Broom, Burton R. Clark, Martin Diamond, Paul Jacobs, Sheldon L. Messinger, Rollin B. Posey, Gertrude J. Selznick,

Herbert A. Simon, and Harold Stein. The fact that I have included some critical comments on Simon's point of view in no way detracts from my great appreciation for his contribution to our common understanding. I am grateful to Dwight Waldo for his persistent and sympathetic encouragement, and to the late Edward Boehm, who gave generously of his long experience and practical insight.

P. S.

Berkeley, California
November, 1956

Contents

ONE

Introduction

The nature and quality of leadership, in the sense of statesmanship, is an elusive but persistent theme in the history of
ideas. Most writers have centered their attention on *political*
statesmen, leaders of whole communities who sit in the high
places where great issues are joined and settled. In our time,
there is no abatement of the need to continue the great
discussion, to learn how to reconcile idealism with expe-
diency, freedom with organization.

But an additional emphasis is necessary. Ours is a pluralist
society made up of many large, influential, relatively autonomous groups. The United States government itself consists
of independently powerful agencies which do a great deal
on their own initiative and are largely self-governing. These,
and the institutions of industry, politics, education, and
other fields, often command large resources; their leaders
are inevitably responsible for the material and psychological
well-being of numerous constituents; and they have become
increasingly *public* in nature, attached to such interests and

dealing with such problems as affect the welfare of the entire community. In our society the need for statesmanship is widely diffused and beset by special problems. An understanding of leadership in both public and private organizations must have a high place on the agenda of social inquiry.

The scientific study of large organizations is certainly not neglected. Much has been learned in the fields of industrial management and public administration. Recent years have seen a lively interest in new approaches to scientific management and in the development of a "theory of organization." Among students of political science, sociology, economics, and business administration there is a steady search for fresh ways of looking at organization, for new "models" to help us achieve a better use of human resources and a more adequate understanding of decision-making.

Much of this interest has quite practical roots. The question most often asked or implied is: How can we make our organizations more *efficient?* How can we improve incentives, communication, and decision-making so as to achieve a smoother-running operation? How can we do the job most surely and at the least cost? This is a necessary and reasonable quest, for there is no doubt that most organizations operate at levels well below their potential capacity.

But does a preoccupation with administrative efficiency lead us to the knottiest and most significant problems of leadership in large organizations? Should efficiency be the central concern of the president of a university or a large business, the head of a government agency or the director of a voluntary association? Are we getting at what is truly basic in the experience of institutional leaders? Are we help-ing to improve the self-knowledge—and thereby the com-petence—of men charged with leadership responsibilities? Are we able to link the development of managerial skills to the larger problems of policy? This essay is an attempt to deal with these questions by exploring the nature of critical decisions and of institutional leadership.

As we ascend the echelons of administration, the analysis of decision-making becomes increasingly difficult, not simply because the decisions are more important or more complex, but because a new "logic" emerges. The logic of efficiency applies most clearly to subordinate units, usually having rather clearly defined operating responsibilities, limited discretion, set communication channels, and a sure position in the command structure. At these lower levels we may expect to find effective use of rather simple devices for increasing efficiency and control; and it is here that scientific techniques of observation and experiment are likely to be most advanced and most successful.

The logic of efficiency loses force, however, as we ap-proach the top of the pyramid. Problems at this level are more resistant to the ordinary approach of management experts. Mechanical metaphors—the organization as a "smooth running machine"—suggest an overemphasis on neat organization and on efficient techniques of administra-tion. It is probable that these emphases induce in the analyst a trained incapacity to observe the interrelation of policy and administration, with the result that the really critical experi-ence of organizational leadership is largely overlooked. This may explain the coolness with which organizational studies are often received by leading administrators, particularly when these studies deal with top command and staff areas. Much of this coolness undoubtedly stems from a natural reaction against proposed changes which may threaten vested interests. Yet there is also a feeling among administrators that the studies offered are naïve and irrelevant, perhaps because they apply a logic which does not adequately reflect the real problems that the administrator himself must face.

The search for a fresh approach to administration has led to a considerable interest in "human relations." This interest has brought about a wider understanding of why people work and how they get along together, particularly in small-scale group settings. The characteristics of small groups, especially the psychological aspects of communication and perception, have received much emphasis. There is no doubt that this work can and does tell us much about the human problems of participation in organizations. But the observer of large enterprises, if he tries to see them whole, is left with a sense of inadequacy. He feels a need to look beyond personal relations to the larger patterns of institutional development. Yet he knows also that no social process can be understood save as it is located in the behavior of individuals, and especially in their perceptions of themselves and each other. The problem is to link the larger view to the more limited one, to see how institutional change is produced by, and in turn shapes, the interaction of individuals in day-to-day situations. The closer we get to the areas of far-reaching decision, the greater is the need for this deeper and more comprehensive understanding of social organization.

The argument of this essay is quite simply stated: *The executive becomes a statesman as he makes the transition from administrative management to institutional leadership.*

This shift entails a reassessment of his own tasks and of the needs of the enterprise. It is marked by a concern for the evolution of the organization as a whole, including its changing aims and capabilities. In a word, it means viewing the organization as an institution. To understand the nature of institutional leadership, we must have some notion of the meaning and significance of the term "institution" itself.

Organizations and Institutions

The most striking and obvious thing about an administrative organization is its formal system of rules and objectives. Here tasks, powers, and procedures are set out according to some officially approved pattern. This pattern purports to say how the work of the organization is to be carried on, whether it be producing steel, winning votes, teaching children, or saving souls. The organization thus designed is a technical instrument for mobilizing human energies and directing them toward set aims. We allocate tasks, delegate authority, channel communication, and find some way of co-ordinating all that has been divided up and parceled out. All this is conceived as an exercise in engineering; it is governed by the related ideals of rationality and discipline.

The term "organization" thus suggests a certain bareness, a lean, no-nonsense system of consciously co-ordinated activities.[1] It refers to an *expendable tool,* a rational instrument engineered to do a job. An "institution," on the other hand, is more nearly a natural product of social needs and pressures—a responsive, adaptive organism. This distinction is a matter of analysis, not of direct description. It does not

[1] C. I. Barnard, *The Functions of the Executive* (Cambridge: Harvard University Press, 1938), p. 73.

mean that any given enterprise must be either one or the other. While an extreme case may closely approach either an "ideal" organization or an "ideal" institution, most living associations resist so easy a classification. They are complex mixtures of both designed and responsive behavior.

When we say that the Standard Oil Company or the Department of Agriculture is to be studied as an institution, we usually mean that we are going to pay some attention to its history and to the way it has been influenced by the social environment. Thus we may be interested in how its organization adapts itself to existing centers of power in the community, often in unconscious ways; from what strata of society its leadership is drawn and how this affects policy; how it justifies its existence ideologically. We may ask what underlying need in the larger community—not necessarily expressed or recognized by the people involved—is filled by the organization or by some of its practices. Thus, the phrase "as a social institution" suggests an emphasis on problems and experiences that are not adequately accounted for within the narrower framework of administrative analysis.

Perhaps a classic example is the analysis of a political constitution as an institution. In such an inquiry the social and cultural conditions (class structure, traditional patterns of loyalty, educational level, etc.) that affect its viability are studied. We see how the formal charter is given life and meaning by the informal "social constitution" in which it is imbedded. When the latter is absent, the constitution is likely to be weak and ineffective. Giving life to a constitution is partly a matter of achieving general consensus regarding proper ways of winning power and making laws.

But much more is also involved. The working of the American constitutional order cannot readily be grasped without understanding the function of the party system in accommodating diverse interests, in blunting the edge of ideological conflicts, in winning for the community a progressive erasure of old issues as new ones arise. Proposals to change the parties into single-minded ideological instruments strike at the institutional basis of the political order. These and similar problems have long been recognized. It is important, however, to make the transition from these great constitutional issues to the less dramatic problems of administration that also arise from the interplay of formal or legal systems and their social environments.

An awareness of the social setting of administrative activity goes beyond "public relations." The latter phrase suggests practices that leave the organization intact, essentially what it has always been, using routine devices for smoothing over difficulties with groups on whom it is dependent. Indeed, much is accomplished in this way. But when an enterprise begins to be more profoundly aware of dependence on outside forces, its very conception of itself may change, with consequences for recruitment, policy, and administrative organization at many levels. As a business, a college, or a government agency develops a distinctive clientele, the enterprise gains the stability that comes with a secure source of support, an easy channel of communication. At the same time, it loses flexibility. The process of institutionalization has set in.

The relation of an organization to the external environment is, however, only one source of institutional experience. There is also an internal social world to be considered. An organization is a group of living human beings. The formal or official design for living never completely accounts for what the participants do. It is always supplemented by what is called the "informal structure," which arises as the individual brings into play his own personality, his special problems and interests. Formal relations co-ordinate roles or specialized activities, not persons. Rules apply to foremen and machinists, to clerks, sergeants, and vice-presidents, yet no durable organization is able to hold human experience to these formally defined roles. In actual practice, men tend to interact as many-faceted persons, adjusting to the daily round in ways that spill over the neat boundaries set by their assigned roles.

The formal, technical system is therefore never more than a part of the living enterprise we deal with in action. The persons and groups who make it up are not content to be treated as manipulable or expendable. As human beings and not mere tools they have their own needs for self-protection and self-fulfillment—needs that may either sustain the formal system or undermine it. These human relations are a great reservoir of energy. They may be directed in constructive ways toward desired ends or they may become recalcitrant sources of frustration. One objective of sound management practice is to direct and control these internal social pressures.

The relations outlined on an organization chart provide a framework within which fuller and more spontaneous human behavior takes place. The formal system may draw upon that behavior for added strength; it will in its turn be subordinated to personal and group egotism. Every official and employee will try to use his position to satisfy his psychological needs. This may result in a gain for the organization if he accepts its goals and extends himself in its interests. But usually, even in the best circumstances, some price is paid in organizational rigidity.

Similarly, when a technically devised organizational unit becomes a social group—a unity of persons rather than of technicians—newly deployable energy is created; but this, too, has inherently divisive and frustrating potentialities. For the unity of persons breaks through the neat confines of rational organization and procedure; it creates new strivings, primarily for the protection of group integrity, that exert an unceasing influence on the formal pattern of delegation and control. This search for security and fulfillment is reflected in the struggle of individuals for place and preferment, in rivalry among units within the organization, and in commitment to ingrained ways of behaving. These are universal features of organizational life, and the problems they raise are perennial ones.

Of these problems, organizational rivalry may be the most important. Such rivalry mobilizes individual egotism while binding it to group goals. This may create a powerful force, threatening the unity of the larger enterprise. Hence it is that within every association there is the same basic constitutional problem, the same need for an accommodative balance between fragmentary group interests and the aims of the whole, as exists in any polity. The problem is aggravated in a special-purpose enterprise because the aims of the whole are more sharply defined, and therefore more vulnerable to divisive activity, than in the natural community.

Organizational rivalry has received a great deal of attention in connection with efforts to unify the United States military establishment. This case is especially instructive, because throughout the discussion the positive value of competition among military agencies has been emphasized. The rivalry in question here does not pertain primarily to combat or low-echelon units, but rather to "headquarters" competition involving the struggle for funds and prestige among the services.

What arrangements, it is asked, will best protect legitimate competition among military services, yet maintain the needed integration of strategic and tactical planning? This broad question depends in turn on others: Who are the key participants in various kinds of organizational rivalry? Of what value is integrated training and should it take place at low levels or at high levels in the command structure? Do weak technical services need special protection against stronger rivals? What can this protection consist of? These and many similar "constitutional" problems arise because of the natural tendency for parochial, self-protective interests of subordinate individuals and groups to be given an undue priority. As in all constitution-making, the problem is to fit this spontaneously generated competition into a framework that will hold it to the interests of the whole.

Once we turn our attention to the emergence of natural social processes within a formal association, and the pressure of these on policy, we are quickly led to a wide range of interesting questions. Thus, the tendency for a group to develop fixed ways of perceiving itself and the world, often unconsciously, is of considerable importance. With this sort of problem in mind, a study of a military intelligence agency, for example, can go beyond the more routine aspects of administrative efficiency. The study should also consider whether any institutional factors affect the ability of the agency *to ask the right questions*. Are its questions related to a general outlook, a tacit image of itself and its task? Is this image tradition-bound? Is it conditioned by long-established organizational practices? Is there a self-restricted outlook due to insecurities that motivate a safe (but narrow and compartmentalized) concept of military intelligence? A study of these problems would explore the conditions under which organizational self-protection induces *withdrawal* from rivalry rather than participation in it. More needs to be known about such pathological withdrawal for it, too—no less than excessive rivalry itself—may frustrate the rational development of organizations and programs.

The dynamics of organizational rivalry—not the mere documentation of its existence—has received very little systematic attention. This is a good example of an area of experience not adequately accounted for within the conceptual framework of administrative analysis. Organizational struggles are usually thought of as adventitious and subversive. This outlook inhibits the development of a body of knowledge *about* organizational rivalry, e.g., stating the conditions and consequences of factional victory, defeat, and withdrawal, or indicating the way external pressures on an organization are reflected in internal controversy.

A similar sensitivity to internal social needs is assumed when we raise the issue in an even more delicate form: Does the conventional organization of military services according to distinctive weapons result in the espousal of self-serving strategies? If there is an intimate relation between strategy and capability, then the strategically unguided development of weapons may create ultimately undesirable commitments to strategies that depend on these weapons. Is it not worth inquiring whether the ability to adapt military planning—including, especially, research and development—to politically significant goals is not inhibited by this organization of the services? The tendency to emphasize methods rather than goals is an important source of disorientation in all organizations. It has the value of stimulating full development of these methods, but it risks loss of adaptability and sometimes results in a radical substitution of means for ends. Leaders may feel more secure when they emphasize the exploitation of technical potentialities, but the difficult task of defining goals and adapting methods to them may be unfulfilled. This is so because the definition of goals requires an appraisal of many co-ordinate objectives —for example, political as well as military—whereas technical development can be more comfortably single-minded.

Taking account of both internal and external social forces, institutional studies emphasize the *adaptive* change and evolution of organizational forms and practices. In these studies the story is told of new patterns emerging and old ones declining, not as a result of conscious design but as natural and largely unplanned adaptations to new situations. The most interesting and perceptive analyses of this type show the organization responding to a problem posed by its history, an adaptation significantly changing the role and character of the organization. Typically, institutional analysis sees legal or formal changes as recording and regularizing an evolution that has already been substantially completed informally.

Thus the emergence of the Operations Division as General Marshall's command post, eclipsing other sections of the General Staff, is an important theme in Cline's institutional history of that agency.[2] In this work we see the contending forces, the changing problems of command, the informal accommodations of interest and power, all contributing to a developing pattern that was largely "in the cards." A similar study of the present Joint Chiefs of Staff organization would attempt to discern the direction of its evolution, keeping in mind as a hypothesis the potential emergence of a single chief for all the services. Such an analysis of a Research and Development Board would take account of the inherent instability of advisory bodies, the pressures for integration into the military command structure and for providing an immediate operational payoff, as well as the possibilities of allaying these pressures without sacrificing the basic character of the agency.[3] Throughout, emphasis is on the group processes at work—how they generate new problems and force new adaptations.

This emphasis on adaptive change suggests that in attempting to understand large and relatively enduring organizations we must draw upon what we know about natural communities. In doing so we are led to consider such matters as the following:

[2] Ray S. Cline, *Washington Command Post: The Operations Division* (Washington, D.C.: Office of the Chief of Military History, Department of the Army, 1951).

[3] Although realistic studies of such organizations are not readily feasible (though not excluded) even at much lower echelons, historical analyses of similar but less "sensitive" agencies can provide a more adequate basis for organization planning. A program of case studies, guided by theoretical sophistication and alertness to significant problems, can provide the data needed. An important beginning along these lines has been made by the Inter-University Case Program under the direction of Harold Stein. See his *Public Administration and Policy Development* (New York: Harcourt, Brace, 1952).

1. The development of administrative ideologies as conscious and unconscious devices of communication and self-defense. Just as doctrinal orthodoxies help natural communities to maintain social order, so, too, in administrative agencies, technical programs and procedures are often elaborated into official "philosophies." These help to build a homogeneous staff and ensure institutional continuity. Sometimes they are created and manipulated self-consciously, but most administrative ideologies emerge in spontaneous and unplanned ways, as natural aids to organizational security. A well-formulated doctrine is remarkably handy for boosting internal morale, communicating the bases for decisions, and rebuffing outside claims and criticisms.

2. The creation and protection of elites. In the natural community elites play a vital role in the creation and protection of values.[4] Similarly, in organizations, and especially those that have or strive for some special identity, the formation of elites is a practical problem of the first importance. Specialized academies, selective recruiting, and many other devices help to build up the self-consciousness and the confidence of present and potential leaders. However, again as in the natural community, counter-pressures work to break down the insulation of these elites and to warp their self-confidence. A problem of institutional leadership, as of statesmanship generally, is to see that elites do exist and function while inhibiting their tendency to become sealed off and to be more concerned with their own fate than with that of the enterprise as a whole. One answer, as in the Catholic Church, is to avoid selectivity in the *choice* of leaders while emphasizing intensive indoctrination in their

4 See pp. 119–130.

training. The whole problem of leadership training, and more generally of forming and maintaining elites, should receive a high priority in scientific studies of organization and policy.

3. The emergence of contending interest-groups, many of which bid for dominant influence in society. The simple protection of their identity, and the attempt to control the conditions of existence, stimulate the normal push and pull of these groups; and the bid for social dominance is reflected in the crises that signify underlying shifts in the distribution of power. The same natural processes go on within organizations, often stimulating the rivalry of formal administrative units, sometimes creating factions that cut across the official lines of communication and command. Here, too, there is normal day-to-day contention, and there is the attempt to become the dominant or "senior" unit, as when a personnel department replaces an accounting division as the source from which general managers are recruited; or when a sales organization comes to dominate the manufacturing organization in product design. These changes cannot, however, be accounted for as simply the products of bureaucratic maneuver. The outcome of the contest is conditioned by a shift in the character and role of the enterprise. Many internal controversies, although stimulated by rather narrow impulses, provide the channels through which broader pressures on the organization are absorbed.

The natural tendencies cited here—the development of defensive ideologies, the dependence of institutional values on the formation and sustaining of elites, the existence of internal conflicts expressing group interests—only illustrate the many elements that combine to form the social structure of an organization. Despite their diversity, these forces have a unified effect. In their operation we see the way group values are formed, for together they define the commitments of the organization and give it a distinctive identity. In other words, to the extent that they are natural communities, organizations have a history; and this history is compounded of discernible and repetitive modes of responding to internal and external pressures. As these responses crystallize into definite patterns, a social structure emerges. The more fully developed its social structure, the more will the organization become valued for itself, not as a tool but as an institutional fulfillment of group integrity and aspiration.

Institutionalization is a *process*. It is something that happens to an organization over time, reflecting the organization's own distinctive history, the people who have been in it, the groups it embodies and the vested interests they have created, and the way it has adapted to its environment. For purposes of this essay, the following point is of special importance: The degree of institutionalization depends on how much leeway there is for personal and group interaction. The more precise an organization's goals, and the more specialized and technical its operations, the less opportunity will there be for social forces to affect its development. A university has more such leeway than most businesses, because its goals are less clearly defined and it can give more free play to internal forces and historical adaptation. But no organization of any duration is completely free of institutionalization. Later we shall argue that leadership is most needed among those organizations, and in those periods of organizational life, where there is most freedom from the determination of decisions by technical goals and methods.

In what is perhaps its most significant meaning, "to institutionalize" is to *infuse with value* beyond the technical requirements of the task at hand. The prizing of social machinery beyond its technical role is largely a reflection of the unique way in which it fulfills personal or group needs. Whenever individuals become attached to an organization or a way of doing things as persons rather than as technicians, the result is a prizing of the device for its own sake. From the standpoint of the committed person, the organization is changed from an expendable tool into a valued source of personal satisfaction. Some manifestations of this process are quite obvious; others are less easily recognized. It is a commonplace that administrative changes are difficult when individuals have become habituated to and identified with long-established procedures. For example, the shifting of personnel is inhibited when business relations become personal ones and there is resistance to any change that threatens rewarding ties. A great deal of energy in organizations is expended in a continuous effort to preserve the rational, technical, impersonal system against such counter-pressures.

Less generally recognized is the effect of this personal involvement on the rational choice of methods and goals. We have already hinted at the importance of "self-images" in, say, restricting the outlook of military-intelligence and similar agencies. These self-images are natural products of organizational experience. They provide the individual with an ordered approach to his day-to-day problems, a way of responding to the world consistently yet involuntarily, in accordance with approved perspectives yet without continuous reference to explicit and formalized rules. This consistent outlook or orientation is indicated when organizational names are applied to individuals as labels for characteristic ways of thinking and working, as when we speak of a "regular army" or a "Foreign Service" man. By long habituation, sometimes also as a result of aggressive indoctrination, the individual absorbs a way of perceiving and evaluating his experience. This reduces his anxiety by lending the world of fact a familiar cast; and it helps assure an easy conformity with established practice.

As in the case of all institutionalization, the development and transmission of self-images is useful but potentially frustrating. To mold the minds of individuals according to a definite pattern creates a homogeneous organization, and this is an enormous aid to communication. A broad context of "understood" meanings ensures that in the performance of assigned tasks the spirit as well as the letter will be observed. Similarly, emotional identification with the organization creates resources of energy that may increase day-to-day effort and, especially, be summoned in times of crisis or threat. But these commitments are costly. They bind the organization to specific aims and procedures, often greatly limiting the freedom of the leadership to deploy its resources, and reducing the capacity of the organization to survive under new conditions.

The test of infusion with value is *expendability*. If an organization is merely an instrument, it will be readily altered or cast aside when a more efficient tool becomes available. Most organizations are thus expendable. When value-infusion takes place, however, there is a resistance to change. People feel a sense of personal loss; the "identity" of the group or community seems somehow to be violated; they bow to economic or technological considerations only reluctantly, with regret. A case in point is the perennial effort to save San Francisco's cable cars from replacement by more economical forms of transportation. The Marine Corps has this institutional halo, and it resists administrative measures that would submerge its identity. In 1950, President Truman became irritated with political pressure favoring Marine Corps membership on the Joint Chiefs of Staff. He wrote a letter calling the Marines the Navy's "police force" and likening their "propaganda machine" to Stalin's. This raised a storm of protest which ended with a presidential apology.

From the standpoint of social systems rather than persons, organizations become infused with value as they come to symbolize the community's aspirations, its sense of identity. Some organizations perform this function more readily and fully than others. An organization that does take on this symbolic meaning has some claim on the community to avoid liquidation or transformation on purely technical or economic grounds. The Marine Corps has this halo far more than other military units and is correspondingly less expendable.

All this is a relative matter and one of degree. With respect to the national community most of the many thousands of organizations in the country are not highly valued for themselves, although certain principles on which they are based, such as free speech or competition, may have deep cultural roots. On the other hand, special groups, such as college alumni, are often urged to keep some organization from dying for lack of support. For the group that participates directly in it, an organization may acquire much institutional value, yet in the eyes of the larger community the organization may be readily expendable.

Both personal and social commitments combine to weaken the purely technical significance of organizations. Beginning as a tool, the organization derives added meaning from the psychological and social functions it performs. In doing so it becomes valued for itself. To be sure, the personal and group bonds that make for institutionalization are not wholly separable. As the individual works out his special problems, seeking his own satisfactions, he helps to tie the organization into the community's institutional network. Personal incentives may spark this absorption, and provide the needed energy; but its character and direction will be shaped by values already existent in the community at large. Similarly, although organizational controversy may be directly motivated by narrow personal and group aims, the contending programs usually reflect ideological differences in the larger arena. In this way, the internal struggle for power becomes a channel through which external environmental forces make themselves felt. This is, indeed, a classic function of the American political party system; but less formal and recognized groupings within administrative organizations follow the same pattern. Organizations do not so much create values as embody them. As this occurs, the organization becomes increasingly institutionalized.

The transformation of expendable technical organizations into institutions is marked by a *concern for self-maintenance.*

A living association blends technical aims and procedures with personal desires and group interests. As a result, various elements in the association have a stake in its continued existence. Moreover, the aims of the organization may require a certain permanence and stability. There is a need to accommodate internal interests and adapt to outside forces, in order to maintain the organization as a "going concern," minimize risks, and achieve long-run as well as short-run objectives. An important sign of this development is that the leaders become security-conscious and are often willing to sacrifice quick returns for the sake of stability. The history of the labor movement is replete with efforts to win union security through provisions for compulsory membership and automatic deduction of dues payments from wages. These objectives look to the long-run maintenance of the union rather than to immediate gains for the members.

There is a close relation between "infusion with value" and "self-maintenance." As an organization acquires a self, a distinctive identity, it becomes an institution. This involves the taking on of values, ways of acting and believing that are deemed important for their own sake. From then on self-maintenance becomes more than bare organizational survival; it becomes a struggle to preserve the uniqueness of the group in the face of new problems and altered circumstances.

To summarize: organizations are technical instruments, designed as means to definite goals. They are judged on engineering premises; they are expendable. Institutions, whether conceived as groups or practices, may be partly engineered, but they have also a "natural" dimension. They are products of interaction and adaptation; they become the receptacles of group idealism; they are less readily expendable.

Some Premises about Leadership

Leadership is not a familiar, everyday idea, as readily available to common sense as to social science. It is a slippery phenomenon that eludes them both. What leaders do is hardly self-evident. And it is likely that much failure of leadership results from an inadequate understanding of its true nature and tasks. Most of this essay will be devoted to identifying and analyzing the chief functions of institutional leadership. By way of introduction, however, it may be helpful to state a few simple guiding ideas here.

1. *Leadership is a kind of work done to meet the needs of a social situation.* Possibly there are some individuals more likely to be leaders than others, possessed of distinguishing personal traits or capacities.[5] Whether or not this is so, we shall here be concerned with leadership as a specialized form of activity, a kind of work or function. Identifying what leaders do certainly bears on (and is perhaps indispensable to) the discovery of requisite personal attributes; but the questions are of a different kind and may be treated separately.

To know the nature of the work done by leaders, we must know something about the social situations they are called upon to handle. This immediately suggests that there must

[5] This problem has received considerable attention, with largely negative but still inconclusive results. See Ralph M. Stogdill, "Personal Factors Associated with Leadership: A Survey of the Literature," *J. Psychology*, 1948, 25: 35–71; also William O. Jenkins, "A Review of Leadership Studies with Particular Reference to Military Problems," *Psychological Bulletin*, 1947, 44: 54–77.

be a very wide variety of activities associated with leadership.[6] However, it does not follow that the *nature* of leadership varies with each social situation. If that were so, there would be nothing determinate about it; its study would be a scientific blind alley. In fact, of course, we must assume that significant leadership patterns are relatively few; and that these patterns are related to *types* of social situations. This means that certain very general activities of leaders—e.g., facilitating communication within the group—reflect equally general characteristics of all human groups; and that the functions of leadership will be understood only as we develop a better understanding of the main types of groups and the recurrent problems they face. In other words, a theory of leadership is dependent on a theory of social organization.

We shall not be concerned here with all leadership, but with leadership in large-scale organizations. This will require some consideration of the nature of such enterprises, including the characteristic problems that arise within them.

---

[6] Indeed, the current literature on this subject, in part as a reaction against the "trait" approach, in part due to the influence of "situational" or "field" theory in social psychology, has made this a central conclusion. Thus Jenkins, *op. cit.,* p. 75, finds: "Leadership is specific to the particular situation under investigation. Who becomes the leader of a given group engaging in a particular activity and what the leadership characteristics are in the given case are a function of the specific situation, including the measuring instruments employed. There is a wide variation in the characteristics of individuals who became leaders in similar situations, and even greater divergence in leadership in different situations." But note the following by Stogdill, *op. cit.,* p. 65: "The evidence suggests that leadership is a relation that exists between persons in a social situation, and that persons who are leaders in one situation may not necessarily be leaders in other situations. Must it then be assumed that leadership is entirely incidental, haphazard, and unpredictable? Not at all. The very studies which provide the strongest arguments for the situational nature of leadership also supply the strongest evidence indicating that leadership patterns as well as non-leadership patterns of behavior are persistent and relatively stable."

It will be necessary to understand the institutional aspects of large-scale organizations, for the central argument will stress the close connection between these aspects and the key functions of leadership. Although institutional leadership must share the general characteristics of all leadership, we shall not deal with the latter problem directly.

2. *Leadership is not equivalent to office-holding or high prestige or authority or decision-making.* It is not helpful to identify leadership with whatever is done by people in high places. The activity we have in mind may or may not be engaged in by those who are formally in positions of authority. This is inescapable if we are to develop a theory that will be useful in diagnosing cases of inadequate leadership on the part of persons in authority. If this view is correct, it means that only some (and sometimes none) of the activities of decision-makers are leadership activities. Here again, understanding leadership requires understanding of a broader social process. If some types of decisions are more closely related to leadership activities than others, we should learn what they are. To this end in this analysis let us make a distinction between "routine" and "critical" decision-making.

3. *Leadership is dispensable.* The word "leadership" has its own halo, easily inviting the tacit assumption that, being a good thing, it is always in order. It may indeed be that all human groups require at all times *some* leadership activities. But if leadership is anything determinate, we should know how to distinguish its presence from its absence; similarly, if there are some social situations that especially require leadership, we should know how to tell them apart from other social situations. The idea is de-

veloped in this essay that leadership is not equally necessary in all large-scale organizations, or in any one at all times, and that it becomes dispensable as the natural processes of institutionalization become eliminated or controlled. This will provide some clues to the general conditions that call for leadership decisions.

These premises emphasize the futility of attempting to understand leadership apart from the broader organizational experience of which it is a phase. A theory of leadership will necessarily reflect the level of sophistication we have reached in the study of organization. We are dealing with an activity, with a function, with work done; we can make no more sense of it than is allowed by our understanding of the field within which that activity takes place.

The Default of Leadership

When institutional leadership fails, it is perhaps more often by default than by positive error or sin. Leadership is lacking when it is needed; and the institution drifts, exposed to vagrant pressures, readily influenced by short-run opportunistic trends. This default is partly a failure of nerve, partly a failure of understanding. It takes nerve to hold a course; it takes understanding to recognize and deal with the basic sources of institutional vulnerability.

One type of default is the failure to set goals. Once an organization becomes a "going concern," with many forces working to keep it alive, the people who run it can readily escape the task of defining its purposes. This evasion stems partly from the hard intellectual labor involved, a labor that often seems but to increase the burden of already onerous daily operations. In part, also, there is the wish to avoid conflicts with those in and out of the organization who would be threatened by a sharp definition of purpose, with its attendant claims and responsibilities. Even business firms find it easy to fall back on conventional phrases, such as that "our goal is to make profit," phrases which offer little guidance in the formulation of policy.

A critique of leadership, we shall argue, must include this emphasis on the leader's responsibility to define the mission of the enterprise. This view is not new. It is important because so much of administrative analysis takes the goal of the organization as given, whereas in many crucial instances this is precisely what is problematic. We shall also suggest that the analysis of goals is itself dependent on an understanding of the organization's social structure. In other words, the purposes we have or can have depend on what we are or what we can be. In statesmanship no less than in the search for personal wisdom, the Socratic dictum—know thyself—provides the ultimate guide.

Another type of default occurs when goals, however neatly formulated, enjoy only a superficial acceptance and do not genuinely influence the total structure of the enterprise. Truly accepted values must infuse the organization at many levels, affecting the perspectives and attitudes of personnel, the relative importance of staff activities, the distribution of authority, relations with outside groups, and many other matters. Thus if a large corporation asserts a wish to change its role in the community from a narrow emphasis on profit-making to a larger social responsibility (even though the ultimate goal remains some combination of survival and profit-making ability), it must explore the implications of such a change for decision-making in a wide variety of organizational activities. We shall stress that the task of building special values and a distinctive competence into the organization is a prime function of leadership.

In this sense, the leader is an agent of institutionalization, offering a guiding hand to a process that would otherwise occur more haphazardly, more readily subject to the accidents of circumstance and history. This is not to say that the leader is free to do as he wishes, to mold the organization according to his heart's desire, restrained only by the quality of his imagination and the strength of his will. Self-knowledge means knowledge of limits as well as of potentialities.

The default of leadership shows itself in an acute form when *organizational* achievement or survival is confounded with *institutional* success. To be sure, no institutional leader can avoid concern for the minimum conditions of continued organizational existence. But he fails if he permits sheer organizational achievement, in resources, stability, or reputation, to become the criterion of his success. A university led by administrators without a clear sense of values to be achieved may fail dismally while steadily growing larger and more secure.

Finally, the role of the institutional leader should be clearly distinguished from that of the "interpersonal" leader. The latter's task is to smooth the path of human interaction, ease communication, evoke personal devotion, and allay anxiety. His expertness has relatively little to do with content; he is more concerned with persons than with policies.

His main contribution is to the efficiency of the enterprise. The institutional leader, on the other hand, *is primarily an expert in the promotion and protection of values.* The interpretation that follows takes this idea as a starting point, exploring its meaning and implications.

TWO

Routine and Critical Decisions

"Decision-making" is one of those fashionable phrases that may well obscure more than it illuminates. It has an air of significance, of reference to important events; and the mere use of the phrase seems to suggest that something definite has been scientifically isolated. But decisions are with us always, at every level of experience, in every organism. The general features of all choice, or of all social choice, may some day be convincingly stated. But it will still be necessary to distinguish the more and the less trivial; and, if there is any order in this phenomenon, to identify some kinds of decision, linking them to the distinctive problems or situations out of which they arise. Here we are concerned with leadership in large organizations. Is there a special kind of experience that underlies and prompts leadership decisions?

A Psychological Analogy

Let us consider the work of two psychologists, each a student of individual behavior. One of these directs his attention to what may be called "routine" psychological processes. He is biologically oriented, usually experimental in method, and interested in the basic psychophysical aspects of behavior. He belongs to the group of psychologists most closely associated with "human engineering," developing useful information on tolerance levels, error, learning, and such related matters as affect the responses of all human beings, in measurable ways, to various types of work and control situations.

Our second man is called a "clinical" psychologist. This term refers directly to method but indirectly to subject-matter. The clinical psychologist is interested in such matters as emotional development and character structure. The methods he uses, such as the depth interview and projective tests, are more obscure and uncertain than those of the experimental psychologist, though the methodological gap is closing. He is more likely to be concerned with disorders, especially those that are "functional" rather than somatic. Above all, the clinical psychologist is distinguished by an interest in the change and growth of total personalities. To the extent that he is concerned with somatic processes, it is not for their own sake, but only as they bear on problems of emotion and character.

The difference between these two broad areas of psychological inquiry is not accidental. The needs of theory and practice created it. But this does not mean that the boundaries are hard and fast. And there are some signs that the difference will ultimately be erased. Our purpose is not to enter the debate among psychologists but to learn from it. This lesson may be that a similar evolution can be expected in the study of organization and decision-making.

The literature of organization analysis is largely concerned with routine processes. "Routine" need not mean unimportant, nor lacking in research interest. Rather, it refers to the solution of day-to-day problems for their own sake. Studies of communication and command channels, work simplification, personnel selection, morale-building techniques, team organization, conference methods, and similar matters, are of this sort. They have to do with the conditions necessary to keep organizations running at efficient levels. They are "technical" in the sense that experts may be employed (and usually are, in large organizations) to take care of these functions, and, indeed, to make them routine. It is in this area that experimental methods are most applicable since small groups of employees may be studied within a controlled design. Here the emphasis is on orderly process, on smooth functioning.

Routine functions include not only the older techniques of management but also those born of the newer "human relations" perspective. We learn from the latter that authority and communication must be broadly understood to take account of the social psychology of obedience, perception, and co-operation. This is the burden of much new thinking and research on organization, including such major contributions as C. I. Barnard's *The Functions of the Executive,* as well as the more experimental studies of group dynamics specialists in social psychology.

If we search for the proper counterpart of the clinical psychologist in organization studies, we shall not find him among the human relations experts. Nothing in the logic of their approach turns them to *the dynamic adaptation of the total organization to internal strivings and external pressures.* But it is just such a "dynamic adaptation" of total personality that defines the main interest of the "clinical" psychologist, particularly if he accepts psychoanalytic premises.[1] Let us inspect the key terms of this formulation a bit more closely, especially the words "dynamic" and "total."

Psychoanalysis is referred to as "dynamic" psychology because it "explains mental phenomena as the result of the interaction and counteraction of forces."[2] This general emphasis on inner need, environmental pressure, and a mediating structure, is shared by other related psychologies, but the Freudians have developed the most complete model. In this view, the personality is an adaptive, equilibrium-seeking organism; but this process is not a smooth continuum of adjustment; there are breaks in the continuum, as, in response to threat, there is a turning inward to reconstruct the self, sometimes in pathological ways. The ego, as "mediator between the organism and the outer world,"[3] draws upon a defensive armory to control inner strivings, as in repression, or to alter the relation between organism and environment, as in regressive withdrawal. These "dynamisms," as they are sometimes called, are associated with persistent modifications of the personality; hence they affect future modes of response.

---

[1] This analogy is of course not offered as proof, but as an aid to reflection; nor does the argument require any literal treatment of organizations as "persons." Rather, we may find that personalities and organizations are particular embodiments of the same *type* of natural system, hence may be analyzed with logically similar tools. Reference to "psychoanalytic psychology" here includes all who work with the main tools developed by Freud, not just to the orthodox Freudians.

[2] Otto Fenichel, *The Psychoanalytic Theory of Neurosis* (New York: Norton, 1945), p. 11.

[3] *Ibid.*, p. 16.

Drawing on general psychoanalytic theory, Erich Fromm distinguishes "static" and "dynamic" adaptation:

> By static adaptation we mean such an adaptation to patterns as leaves the whole character structure unchanged and implies only the adoption of a new habit. An example of this kind of adaptation is the change from the Chinese habit of eating to the Western habit of using fork and knife. A Chinese coming to America will adapt himself to this new pattern, but this adaptation in itself will have little effect on his personality; it does not arouse new drives or character traits.[4]

This may be compared with the idea of routine psychological processes suggested above. Static adaptation is not static, strictly speaking: it is, one might say, "everyday" dynamics. It is routine learning, and the study of it centers on such factors as motivation, practice, etc. It is ordinary, responsive behavior, subject to such normal tendencies as stimulus generalization. Most human responses are of this routine sort. It is natural that, wherever the training and control of large numbers is involved, as in industrial or military life, the students of these processes will have the major role.

Yet certain critical areas of experience belong to a different realm:

> By dynamic adaptation we refer to the kind of adaptation that occurs, for example, when a boy submits to the commands of his strict and threatening father—being too much afraid of him to do otherwise—and becomes a "good" boy. While he adapts himself to the necessities of the situation, something happens in him. He may develop an intense hostility against his father, which he represses, since it would be too dangerous to express

[4] Erich Fromm, *Escape from Freedom* (New York: Rinehart, 1941), p. 15.

it or even to be aware of it. This repressed hostility, however, though not manifest, is a dynamic factor in his character structure. It may create new anxiety and thus lead to still deeper submission; it may set up a vague defiance, directed against no one in particular but rather toward life in general. While here, too, as in the first case, an individual adapts himself to certain external circumstances, this kind of adaptation creates something new in him, arouses new drives and new anxieties. Every neurosis is an example of this dynamic adaptation.[5]

"Dynamic" here connotes more than simple activity, change, or growth. It suggests certain impelling forces that have a quite different origin and role from the routine tissue tensions of hunger, toothache, and sex. In dynamic adaptation, there is no simple one-to-one relation between an isolated stimulus and its response, a particular drive and its satisfaction, even if one accepts the idea that to some degree the total organism is implicated in all responsive behavior. The point is not the degree of involvement, but the reconstruction of need, the change in posture and strategy, the commitment to new types of satisfaction.

The relevance of these remarks for organizational theory is not far to seek. "Static adaptation" occurs in organizations as well as in personalities. The day-to-day functioning of the organization requires the continuous solution of problems. For the most part, the existing structure—both the informal human relations and the more formal patterns of communication and control—is competent to meet issues as they arise *without internal crisis*. As the daily work proceeds, changes occur, but normally these do not significantly affect the nature of the enterprise or its leadership.

[5] *Ibid.*, pp. 15–16.

Even changes in top personnel may not be significant, if succession is orderly and fundamental policy is firmly established. The corporation grinds out sales and products; the union continues its ceaseless round of negotiations; the government agency extends approved services to assigned publics. Within broad limits, we sometimes say, these large organizations "run themselves"; yet we understand that this holds only for routine activity. In organizational life, just as in individual behavior, this routine functioning and adaptation is quantitatively preponderant. And the proper tooling of everyday activity is a legitimate and necessary preoccupation of management.

Yet in organizations, too, it is plainly necessary to focus attention on dynamics, to study less routine kinds of adaptation. There is a vital sector of organizational experience that cannot be understood as simple problem-solving in which the organization remains essentially intact. Rather, in this sector we find such adaptations of leadership to the interplay of internal and external forces as result in basic institutional changes. This is the area of "character-defining" commitments, which affect the organization's capacity to control its own future behavior. The range of discretion becomes limited, often in unanticipated ways; or it may be significantly broadened. For example, a government agency may adapt itself to a potentially hostile clientele by appointing representatives of the clientele to the agency staff. This has far-reaching consequences for policy, and is not understandable as simple "economic" personnel procurement.

In organizations, "dynamic adaptation" takes place in the shadowy area where administration and policy meet. We must take this, not in the obvious sense that administrative devices execute and form policy, but rather in the sense that organizational processes profoundly influence the kinds of policy that can be made, and policy in turn shapes the machinery of organization in ways that cannot be accounted for on the premises of efficient functioning. At the same time, this is precisely the area of "critical experience" upon which we wish to focus.

When we discuss the bearing of military unification on strategy, the social composition of administrative staffs, the restrictive consequences of administrative alliances, the abandonment of old agencies for new ones, the relation of autonomy to the defense of a program, the unorthodox administrative practices of Franklin Roosevelt, and similar matters, we find ourselves outside the area where administration can be made routine. We are squarely in the field where leadership counts and where managerial *expertise* is of secondary importance.

The term "leadership" connotes critical experience rather than routine practice. This is suggested in the following comment by Barnard:

> The overvaluation of the apparatus of communication and administration is opposed to leadership and the development of leaders. It opposes leadership whose function is to promote appropriate adjustment of ends and means to new environmental conditions, because it opposes change either of status in general or of established procedures and habitual routine. This overvaluation also discourages the development of leaders by retarding the progress of the abler men and by putting an excessive premium on routine qualities.[6]

[6] C. I. Barnard, *Organization and Management* (Cambridge: Harvard University Press, 1948), pp. 240 f.

However, it is easy to overemphasize the *personal* element. While personal qualities are important, and reflect differences in self-conception, too much attention to them may obscure the essential distinction. Even the person free of "routine qualities" may in fact be performing a routine function if he devotes his main energy to greasing the wheels of organization, albeit in human terms. In thinking of leadership, we too often have in mind the personal relation of leader and follower, especially as it involves such psychological mechanisms as identification. This emphasis leads us away from the role of leadership in the making of critical decisions.

It is in the realm of policy—including the areas where policy-formation and organization-building meet—that the distinctive quality of institutional leadership is found. Ultimately, this is the quality of statesmanship which deals with current issues, not for themselves alone but according to their long-run implications for the role and meaning of the group. Group leadership is far more than the capacity to mobilize personal support; it is more than the maintenance of equilibrium through the routine solution of everyday problems; it is the function of the leader-statesman—whether of a nation or a private association—to define the ends of group existence, to design an enterprise distinctively adapted to these ends, and to see that that design becomes a living reality. These tasks are not routine; they call for continuous self-appraisal on the part of the leaders; and they may require only a few critical decisions over a long period of time. "Mere speed, frequency, and vigor in coming to decisions may have little relevance at the top executive level, where a man's basic contribution to the enterprise may turn on his making two or three significant decisions a year." [7] This basic contribution is not always aided by the traits often associated with psychological leadership, such as aggressive self-confidence, intuitive sureness, ability to inspire.

The Concept of Organization Character

Our general perspective may be clarified further if we continue the psychological analogy. In particular, the process of "character-formation" seems worth exploring for the insights it may yield to students of institutionalization and critical decision-making. When we have seen the connection between these two phenomena we shall be in a better position to analyze the nature and tasks of institutional leadership.

The idea of "character" as used by personality analysts is not altogether clear, but its usefulness is scarcely in doubt. There seems to be general agreement on four attributes.

First, character is a *historical* product. "The character as a whole," writes Fenichel, "reflects the individual's historical development." [8] Character is the "ego's habitual ways of reacting." In this sense every individual has a unique character.

Second, character is in some sense an *integrated* product, as is suggested by the term "character-structure." There is a discoverable pattern in the way the ego is organized; and the existence of such a pattern is the basis of character analysis.

Third, character is *functional,* in the sense that it is no mere accidental accretion of responsive patterns. Character

[7] E. P. Learned, D. N. Ulrich, and D. R. Booz, *Executive Action*, Harvard University Graduate School of Business Administration, Boston, 1951, p. 57.

[8] Otto Fenichel, *The Psychoanalytic Theory of Neurosis* (New York: Norton, 1945), p. 470.

development fulfills a task set by the requirements of personality organization: the defense of the individual against inner and outer demands which threaten him. "Biologically speaking, character formation is an autoplastic function. In the conflict between instinct and frustrating outer world, and motivated by the anxiety arising from this conflict, the organism erects a protection mechanism between itself and the outer world." [9] Whatever the special content of varying theories of character-formation, they share an emphasis on the *reconstruction of the self* as a way of solving anxiety-laden problems.

Fourth, character is *dynamic* in that it generates new strivings, new needs and problems. It is largely through the identification of these needs that diagnosis proceeds, as when the discovery of excessive dependency or aggressiveness suggests that the patient has a particular type of character-structure.

Now let us compare these attributes of character with the discussion above of how organizations become institutions. The following points were emphasized there:

1. The technical, rational, impersonal, task-oriented formal system (the "organization") is conditioned by the responsive interaction of persons and groups.

2. In the course of time, this responsive interaction is patterned. A social structure is created. This patterning is *historical*, in that it reflects the specific experiences of the particular organization; it is *functional* in that it aids the organization to adapt itself to its internal and external social environment; and it is *dynamic*, in that it generates new and active forces, especially internal interest-groups

[9] Wilhelm Reich, *Character-Analysis*, New York, 1949, p. 159.

made up of men committed to particular jobs or policies.

3. Organizations become institutions as they are *infused with value*, that is, prized not as tools alone but as sources of direct personal gratification and vehicles of group integrity. This infusion produces a distinct identity for the organization. Where institutionalization is well advanced, distinctive outlooks, habits, and other commitments are unified, coloring all aspects of organizational life and lending it a *social integration* that goes well beyond formal co-ordination and command.

The study of organizational character-formation is, then, a phase of institutional analysis. Here the emphasis is on the embodiment of values in an organizational structure through the elaboration of commitments—ways of acting and responding that can be changed, if at all, only at the risk of severe internal crisis. As in the case of individuals, the emergence of organizational character reflects the irreversible element in experience and choice. A great deal of management practice, as in the hiring of personnel, may be viewed as an effort to hold down the number of irreversible decisions that must be made. On the other hand, a wise management will readily limit its own freedom, accepting irreversible commitments, when the basic values of the organization and its direction are at stake. The acceptance of irreversible commitments is the process by which the character of an organization is set.

We have suggested that "critical" experience is closely related to organizational self-definition and self-reconstruction. This experience reflects the "open-endedness" of organizational life—the existence of alternative ways of responding and changing. Critical experience calls for leadership.

Experience is less critical, and leadership is more dispensable, when the range of alternatives is limited by rigid technical criteria. The more limited and defined the task, the more readily can technical criteria prevail in decision-making. That is one reason why critical experience increases as we ascend the echelons of administration, where decisions based on broader interests must be made. But when the organization is not so limited, when it has the leeway to respond in alternative ways, there is room for character-formation, which enters to give structure to precisely this area of freedom.[10] Hence leadership, character, and critical decision-making are linked as aspects of the same basic phenomenon: the institutionalization of organizational life.

Perhaps the most obvious indicator of organizational character as a palpable reality is the abandonment of old organizations and the creation of new ones when changes in general orientation seem required. A new program does not always call for a new organization, but where a new point of view is to be embodied, there is often recourse to a fresh start. The fear is that the character of the old organization will create resistances to the full development of the new program. In practical terms, this usually means that the

[10] Cf. Karl W. Deutsch, "Communication in Self-Governing Organizations," in *Freedom and Authority in Our Time* (New York: Harper, 1953): "The importance of memory is the greater, and the effects of its loss the more severe, because a functioning memory implies the probability of eventual *individuation*. Two organizations might set out with exactly the same structure, and yet the different experiences from the outside world would eventually produce different stocks of memories in each, and eventually different kinds of behavior even in the presence of identical stimuli. Then such organizations might function in some respects similarly to individuals with peculiarities of personality; and as their memory-guided behavior might influence their intake of subsequent memories, such organizations might be capable of considerable internal evolution" (p. 275).

new program, even if accepted in good faith, may be threatened by personnel or budgetary procedures, and by many other operating routines that are uncongenial to it. An organization requiring considerable flexibility in personnel practice may find itself seriously hampered as part of a larger enterprise that must, considering the interests of the whole, enforce more rigid standards. Or, where long-established habits of work prevail, a new program may find itself quickly redefined into terms that sustain the received patterns. Issues of this sort were involved when the Roosevelt administration set up many new agencies, as in agriculture, instead of channeling new programs through existing organizations.

Character as Distinctive Competence

In studying character we are interested in the *distinctive competence or inadequacy* that an organization has acquired. In doing so, we look beyond the formal aspects to examine the commitments that have been accepted in the course of adaptation to internal and external pressures.

For purposes of illustration, let us examine briefly two rather different organizational experiences which have been previously investigated and reported, and in which the phenomenon considered here was studied. We may then consider some further applications and theoretical implications.

1. *Policy and character in the TVA experience.* In a study of the Tennessee Valley Authority,[11] the policy of channeling a federal program through local agencies was examined.

[11] Philip Selznick, *TVA and the Grass Roots* (Berkeley and Los Angeles: University of California Press, 1949).

In particular, the agricultural activities of the Authority were carried out in co-operation with the Extension Services of the land-grant colleges in the seven Valley states. This co-operation was extensive; in effect, the Extension Service organizations became the operating arm of the TVA in the agricultural field. In assessing the consequences of this arrangement, it was necessary to inquire into such commitments of the Extension Services as (1) might affect the way in which the TVA agricultural program was administered, and (2) might have a broader influence on policy-making in the TVA as a whole.

The "character" of the Extension Service was reflected in the following set of related commitments: (1) The involvement of the county agricultural agent in "courthouse" politics; (2) the intimate relation between the Extension Service and the American Farm Bureau Federation; (3) a tendency of the extension agents to deal with the relatively more prosperous elements of the local farm population and to reflect certain dominant attitudes, such as those toward farm tenancy; (4) a shift in the role of the Extension Service from a primarily educational emphasis to the acceptance of responsibility for "action" programs. These and related commitments, it was found, significantly affected the ability of the TVA to achieve an agricultural program that would be free of restrictive pressures. In addition, the TVA's commitment to the Extension Service involved it in the national struggle for control of the U.S. agricultural programs, drawing it into the Farm Bureau camp. Further, the commitment created a group *inside* TVA that defended general Extension Service attitudes and objectives and successfully exerted pressure on other TVA programs, e.g., forcing revision of the policy reserving a strip of land around the reservoirs for public access and for recreation and conservation activities.

On the other hand, the TVA purchased a considerable advantage with these concessions. It gained the support of important local interests and of a powerful national lobby. These defended not only the agricultural program but TVA as a whole. In this way, by modifying its agricultural program and certain broad social policies, the Authority was able to ward off threatened dismemberment and to gain time for the successful development of its key activity —the expansion of electric power facilities.

The critical decisions taken here—not necessarily consciously—had little to do with efficient operation as such.[12] They were intimately related to the way the Extension Services had become *institutionalized* and had absorbed commitments to personnel, practices, and group interests. These commitments, taken together, formed the relevant character of the Extension Services. This in turn defined the capacity of these agencies to aid the TVA's adaptation to its area of operations; but it also made them something other than innocent collaborators in the administration of a technical program. Both advantages and disadvantages for

[12] However, even apparently routine matters of administrative procedure had to be assessed against the general background discussed here. Thus the choice between a contractual arrangement that would call for a lump-sum grant by TVA to the colleges, as against reimbursement for detailed items of expenditure, could not be understood apart from the aim of giving the Extension Services maximum freedom. The policy adopted—of reimbursement for detailed items—though superficially suggesting a measure of control by the Authority, in fact was congenial to the loose arrangement desired. A lump-sum grant procedure invites inspection of other kinds of detail, including work planning and fiscal controls within the recipient agency, to say nothing of the possibility of instituting a requirement that the colleges match sums contributed by the TVA to the co-operative program.

TVA derived from the institutional aspects of the Extension Services.

The emergent character of the TVA itself, of course, was significantly influenced by its own interaction with the land-grant college system. As a result of this interaction, the Authority absorbed commitments to an ideology and to specific institutions that modified its role as a New Deal agency.

2. *Bolshevik character-definition.* A study of the Bolshevik type of party also led to the investigation of organizational character-formation.[13] The distinctive competence of the Bolshevik "combat" party lies in its ability to transform members of a voluntary association into disciplined and deployable agents. This requires the building of an organization that can be oriented to the continuous conquest of power in all areas of social life. Such an organization cannot be created by verbal resolutions alone. Special measures must be taken to "Bolshevize" the organization, that is, to see that its own commitments—to structure, personnel, and doctrine—are so firmly set as to be virtually irreversible.

One problem confronting the Communists over a number of years was the repudiating of socialist methods of organization and activity. The Communist organizations were formed as offshoots of the socialist parties. They brought with them a heritage which had to be eradicated if a new type of organization adapted to the continuous struggle for power—especially in industry rather than in the electoral arena—was to be built. These alterations in-

[13] Philip Selznick, *The Organizational Weapon* (New York: McGraw-Hill, 1952).

cluded an overhauling of the party structure itself, to do away with the older territorial divisions adapted to the running of election campaigns, and to substitute a much more flexible party unit capable of facilitating control in key industries. In addition, the older social-democratic attitude toward leadership was changed. The status of the full-time party official was greatly enhanced, and measures were instituted to control middle-class leaders whose life-commitment to the party was not complete. This reorientation could not be simply formal, but demanded a restructuring of the attitudes and actions of the membership. The habits of political activity are not easily altered when established in the course of years of effort; so, too, with the attempt to increase the stature of the full-time official and to alter the relation of the ideological leader to the party. These attitudes toward leadership and proper methods of work help to form the character of the organization as a whole.

Another aspect of organizational character-definition is control over the *social composition* of the membership. It is evident that where the class, family, sectional, or ethnic origins of personnel are uncontrolled, unanticipated consequences for decision-making may ensue. Organizations that are self-conscious about their characters—an officers' corps, an elite school, etc.—normally attempt to control composition by being selective, so that only persons having appropriate social origins are accepted. The Communists are likewise concerned about composition but are not able to be completely selective. As a consequence, they must devise special measures for the reorientation of personnel whose origins may raise doubts as to reliability and utility. Such doubts arise especially in the relation of the party to members recruited from among doctors, writers, teachers, and other professionals. The party meets this organizational problem by *recruiting selectively* among professionals, establishing more rigorous criteria for admission than in the case of industrial workers; by *intensive education,* insisting on a compulsory schedule of indoctrination through discussion groups, party schools, and literature oriented to intellectuals; and by involving the intellectual in *mass work,* e.g., by assigning him to work with a group of Communists in a trade-union, acting as secretary or educational director. These practices reflect the need to shape the commitments of personnel where these are not already established by the individual's earlier life-experience. The problem is especially acute, of course, for any organization, such as the Bolshevik type of party, which seeks to induce an esoteric reorientation and therefore cannot depend on the ordinary machinery of education in the community at large.

The TVA and Bolshevik experiences are of course widely different. Yet in each there is an emergent institutional pattern that decisively affects the competence of an organization to frame and execute desired policies. Commitments to ways of acting and responding are built into the organization. When integrated, these commitments define the "character" of the organization. Of the two cases, the Bolshevik experience is perhaps the more instructive, for it points to a distinctive *type,* not simply a unique accretion of rigidities or capabilities. The Bolshevik type of party has a *generalized* character as well as a historical uniqueness. It is a new *kind* of party, a "combat" party, one capable of deploying members as disciplined agents in a far-flung struggle for power.

The point may be further clarified if we compare the Democratic and Republican parties in the United States. In the same sense that each individual has a unique character, these parties have historically conditioned differences. Though they are different, these parties share significant capabilities and limitations. They are parties of the same *type*—committed to electoral victory in the short run, decentralized, capable of absorbing new ideas and social forces, incapable of making many demands upon a weakly involved party membership.

When we speak of "commitment" here we mean more than merely verbal assent or even ideological attachment. Thus "commitment to the short run" refers to the actual interests of those who man the party organization—their personal stake in victory or defeat. It is conceivable that a long period out of power may shift control of one of the parties into the hands of men who, though they might like to win, do not really have to win. Such men might be able to afford the luxury of losing elections while retaining the comforting purity of the party leadership and its principles. A shift of this kind at the local level would tend to change the nature of the party from a majority-forming agency, receptive to change and compromise, into a more narrowly ideological instrument.

The Bolshevik "combat" party is a different kind of institution. It is not committed to short-run electoral victory; it establishes maximal control over the individual, creating a membership deployable outside of politics proper (e.g., in trade-unions); it achieves a tight doctrinal unity and is incapable of any but tactical accommodations. Though each is a political organization dedicated to the achievement of power, it is impossible without severe distortion to classify the Bolshevik type of party with the parties of Western parliamentarism.

In each of these cases, we have emphasized the emergence of special capabilities and limitations as institutionalization proceeds. And indeed, as a practical matter, the assessment of organizations necessarily scrutinizes this element of competence or disability. During the controversy over military unification referred to above, the Navy Department emerged as the defender of subtle institutional values and tried many times to formulate the distinctive characteristics of the various services. The naval leaders emphasized the special sensitivities each had acquired as a result of long historical development. Thus in the published diary of the first Secretary of Defense we read:

[Gruenther] made the observation that there was a fundamental difference in thinking between Army and Navy on the question of a Staff versus Committee system of arriving at decisions. I concurred, but I said the difference went deeper than that—for example, the vast difference in the conduct of war on land masses and the kind of war that was fought in the Pacific; the inherent organizational differences between Army and Navy derived from the fact that the smallest unit the Army could employ was a division, whereas the Navy was accustomed to operating either a single PT or a task force of a thousand ships, and for that reason had to be flexible. Gruenther admitted that there was this basic difference, both as regards the character of war and the character of organization.[14]

Other Navy spokesmen attempted to distinguish between the Army as a "manpower" organization and the Navy as a finely adjusted system of technical, engineering skills—a "machine-centered" organization. Faced with what it perceived as a mortal threat, the Navy became highly self-conscious about its distinctive competence, although many of the formulations offered had the ring of partisan improvisation.

The idea of distinctive competence is not necessarily restricted to the outcome of an organization's peculiar adaptation to its own special purposes and programs. A somewhat more general competence may develop, as when we say that a firm is good at marketing but less successful in production. Many organizations, though they have different objectives, face similar problems and become adapted to solving those problems. Thus some groups have in common the need to mobilize and control volunteer units, whether for fund-raising, political action, or fire-fighting. Analyzing these common problems may yield a better way of classifying organizations than focusing attention on similarities in structure or in aims.

The distinctive competence to do a *kind* of thing is in question when we ask whether an agency is well adapted to carrying out an "action" program. This has little to do with routine administrative efficiency; rather, it reflects the general orientation of personnel, the flexibility of organiza-

[14] Walter Millis (ed.), *The Forrestal Diaries* (New York: Viking, 1951), pp. 314–315. Note also the assessment of general orientation in John J. McCloy's comment on Air Force attitudes toward close air support, quoted herein on p. 72.

tional forms, and the nature of the institutional environment to which the organization is committed. In the mid-thirties, the assessment of the Extension Service's capacity to serve as a field force for new Federal agricultural programs turned on these matters, an assessment that led to the creation of new organizations in the belief that these would be better adapted to an aggressive program of government intervention.

The debate over the Department of State's suitability as a psychological warfare agency has required a similar appraisal, involving such questions as: (*a*) Does the training of Foreign Service officers result in a passive orientation, a disposition to wait for something to happen rather than to go out to meet it? (*b*) Is the Department able to maintain enough freedom from the pressure of day-to-day opinion to enable it to develop strategic plans objectively? Efforts to retain the Foreign Service as a distinctive unit having claims to esoteric skills probably reflect this concern. (*c*) Can the same leadership that must develop a policy of accommodation to hostile powers create the organizational conditions necessary for a dynamic program of "psychological warfare"? (*d*) Given the need for close integration between foreign policy decisions and propaganda, will this integration be better achieved with a psychological warfare organization *inside* the Department of State—hence theoretically "closer" to policy-formation—or do conflicts of function within the Department make it likely that performance will be better when the psychological warfare agency is independent of the Department and able to exert pressure upon it? In other words, do the commitments of the Department to established outlooks and procedures provide a congenial environment for an organization that must mobilize information and skills for day-to-day action on a broad front, of which diplomatic negotiations are only one sector?

In a quite different field, the "action" potentialities of the National Association for the Advancement of Colored People have received some attention.[15] The NAACP has scored its most brilliant successes in the courts, culminating in the Supreme Court ruling against segregation in the public schools. It has not engaged in much mass agitational activity, nor has it been effectively primed for the problems of mobilization and direction which such activity entails. On the whole, the NAACP has tended to follow rather than lead in the field of mass action. The March on Washington Movement during World War II, the mass pressure for employment of Negroes in Harlem stores, and the bus boycott of 1956 in Montgomery, Alabama, were characteristically organized outside of the NAACP.

The weakness of the organization as a "direct action" group stems from and is reflected in its internal structure as well as in its relations to both the Negro and white communities. Structurally the NAACP has been very much a "headquarters" enterprise; its loosely bound members have functioned mainly as a "tax" base to support the headquarters, much as a government agency is supported by the general taxpayer. Relatively little attention has been paid to local organization and only a few paid regional directors have been employed. Moreover, the organization has close ties to the middle-class white community, from

[15] See Paul Jacobs, "The NAACP's New Direction," *The New Republic,* July 16, 1956.

which it gains money, status, and political allies. Within the Negro community, its base has also been primarily middle class. The result is an organization which cannot easily be called upon to engage in unaccustomed types of action or to support "precipitous" policies.

There were, to be sure, very good reasons for this development, including the exposed position of local people, their dependence on a protected headquarters, and the availability of the courts as channels for constructive change. But whatever the reasons, the emergence of a distinctive competence to win community support for legal action has probably carried with it a distinctive incompetence to take the lead in situations calling for mass action. An effort to change this basic orientation would require substantial changes in leadership and organizational structure, a much greater emphasis on member education, and significant moves to find a new pattern of alliance within both white and Negro communities.

The assessment of industrial firms also requires study of distinctive capabilities and limitations. For example, a commitment to quality of product may be an important determinant of organizational character or institutionalization.

The first boats made by Gar Wood were high quality craft, made of the finest materials by master boat builders. Later, the company decided to mass-produce a comparatively low cost speed boat for wide distribution. It developed that the entire organization found itself unable to cope with the effort to shift commitments. Workmen and shop supervisors alike continued to be preoccupied with high cost quality craftsmanship. Members of the selling staff, too, could not shift emphasis from "snob appeal" to price appeal. The quality commitment was so strong that an entirely new division—operating in a separate plant hundreds of miles away and therefore recruiting from a different labor market—had to be created to do the job successfully.[16]

A radical step was needed to provide organizational conditions congenial to the execution of a new policy. This was not a problem to which narrow criteria of organization engineering could be applied. It required an assessment of the built-in capabilities and limitations of the organization, that is, of its character as shaped by institutionalization.

In his study of the retailing activities of Sears, Roebuck and Co., Moore has used a similar concept of organization character. "The character of a store," he writes, "just like the character of an individual, is determined by what it does, but obviously what it does depends on the limits of its own resources, how it fits into the already established community, and how it comes to be regarded by the general public. All of this is a mutually interacting complex, involving growth, development, and fortuitous circumstances as well as conscious planned effort."[17]

Moore reminds us that Sears' retailing grew out of an already established mail-order business:

Prior to the birth of retailing, Sears, Roebuck and Company was capable of selling a quarter of a billion dollars worth of merchandise *sight unseen*. It was nationally known; and it al-

[16] From unpublished notes by the late Edward Boehm, formerly a Vice-President of Gar Wood Industries.
[17] David G. Moore, "Managerial Strategies and Organization Dynamics in Sears Retailing" (Unpublished doctoral dissertation, University of Chicago, 1954), p. 45. For a discussion of policy and organization character, see Selznick, *TVA and the Grass Roots*, pp. 181 ff.

ready had an institutional quality. Opening up Sears stores was like bringing the catalogue to life. . . . While Sears retailing took advantage of the Sears name, it also geared itself to the growth and development of large urban centers and the increasing use of the automobile. The development of the parking-lot, single-stop, family store located in an easily accessible place away from the center of town was Sears' strategic answer to the problem of competition in the central shopping district. It simply took advantage of the growth of the city and the development of the family automobile. More than this, the outlying location fitted its character as a retail store much better than competing in a downtown location. A Sears retail store is not typically a dominant store like Marshall Field's or J. L. Hudson's. Its character lies somewhere between a large neighborhood store and a downtown department store. Executives of large retailing establishments like those connected with the Associated Merchandising Corporation do not regard Sears as a department store in the full sense of the word. The distinction is not quite clear, but perhaps they are making reference to the fact that Sears is not, typically, a downtown store, handling a complete line of merchandise, and doing its own buying, or, for that matter carrying its whole merchandising and sales promotion load. It is more akin to an expanded auto store or electrical accessory store from the AMC point of view.[18]

The formation of an institution is marked by the making of value commitments, that is, choices which fix the assumptions of policymakers as to the nature of the enterprise—its distinctive aims, methods, and role in the community. These character-defining choices are not made verbally; they may not even be made consciously. When such com-

[18] Moore, *op. cit.*, pp. 49–50.

mitments are made, the values in question are actually built into the social structure, as in the case of the Gar Wood craftsmen just cited, or when the special weight or status accorded to one division in a business or government agency reflects and sustains a major policy decision.

Policy and Critical Decision

Decisions affecting institutional development are critical decisions. When made consciously they reflect or constitute "policy" in its traditional sense. However, the word "policy" is often used rather loosely in administrative circles and is applied to any rule or course of action designed to guide specific decisions. Thus we may hear of vacation policies, or promotion policies, irrespective of whether or not these bear on the creation or preservation of key values. Such usage is unfortunate to the extent that it blurs the distinction between routine and critical experience.

Among students of public administration, the need to distinguish analytically between policy-making and policy-serving decisions has long been recognized. This is reflected in the separation of "policy" and "administration," the former denoting aims and rules formulated by a legislature or other political body, the latter reserved for technical, executive, policy-serving functions. There is growing awareness, however, that this separation of policy and administration can obscure the truth.[19] At the same time, the term "basic policy" suggests something more than mere permanence; it has long-run implications for the organization,

[19] See Dwight Waldo, *The Administrative State* (New York: Ronald, 1948), pp. 123 ff.; also Albert Lepawsky, *Administration* (New York: Knopf, 1949), Chap. III.

not merely in being permanent, but even more in deciding central aims and distinctive methods.

In asserting the continuity of policy and administration, we are saying that certain organizational practices can enter the critical experience of leadership. These practices and the attitudes associated with them help to shape the key values in the organization, and especially the distribution of the power to affect these values.[20]

1. Decisions regarding the *recruitment of personnel* may become part of critical experience. This occurs when selection must take account of more than technical qualification, as when leading individuals are chosen for their personal commitment to precarious aims or methods. Not only cabinet ministers, but the heads of quite subordinate sections of an organization may be screened in this way. In business it may be important to have an executive who is "sales-minded" or "research-minded" or "production-minded." It may at times be useful to recruit whole staffs from a particular social milieu, in order to increase the chances that a given set of policies will become meaningful and effective guides to behavior. Where functions can be narrowly and technically defined, this type of recruitment is often unnecessary, and recruitment policy will not occupy a central place in the attention of leadership. But where the social composition of the staff significantly affects the interplay of policy and administration, personnel selection cannot be dealt with as routine management practice.

[20] "Value" here is not used in a very general sense, such as "object of any interest," but rather to denote something which in the given organization is taken as an end in itself. Note also that not all power distribution is relevant, but only that which can affect these values. This excludes the controlled delegation of authority, save as incidental discretion may influence the emergent character of the organization.

2. *Training of personnel* may also enter the critical experience of leadership. Where implementation of policy depends to any considerable extent on the attitudes and ways of thinking of personnel, an effort must be made to translate policy into an "organization doctrine" and to inculcate these ideas wherever necessary. Indoctrination becomes critically important when policies are insecure. This occurs if policies are new and meet resistance—as when union recognition and collective bargaining require the education of foremen—or when a policy based on the integration of ideas (e.g., politico-military) is likely to be emasculated because those ideas are only superficially accepted or understood. Policymakers must take account of the capacity of a given organization to absorb a point of view. The reconstruction of an organization to make it an adequate vehicle for an insecure or precarious policy has its own logic, demanding the close attention of leadership.

3. Organization-building is also intimately related to policy in the establishment of a system for *the representation of internal group interest.* The function of a leader, at whatever level, is in part to promote and defend the interests of his unit. When freedom to do this is allowed, the top leadership, responsible for the organization as a whole, can feel assured that the values entrusted to the unit will be effectively promoted and defended. This must, of course, be combined with effective co-ordination. But co-ordination involves more than harmonious action. It also consists of "constitutional" procedures for creating balanced representation and for adjudicating conflicts. Such conflicts, given a basic loyalty to the whole enterprise, are taken as normal rather than pathological. They are not routine, for

they reflect the open-endedness of institutional life. Organization controversy—whatever its real source—tends to raise issues that bear heavily on the evolution of key values, if for no other reason than to justify the struggle for group prestige and personal power. Indeed, a system of internal "checks and balances" is in part a way of insuring that policy issues are automatically thrust to the top for scrutiny and action. The problems of co-ordination, seen as the interplay of values, power, and organizational practice, form a major part of the critical experience of institutional leadership.

4. *Co-operation with other organizations* is another field of administrative action fraught with policy implications. Co-operation threatens a loss of control, since commitments in action tend to spill over the limits of verbal agreement. Indeed, a proposal for (or resistance to) co-operation very often reflects a strategy for organizational aggrandizement or protection at least as much as it does an interest in the program to be furthered. Within limits, this is no sign of evil or selfish design, but a natural function of leadership. Proposals for co-operation in a particular area must be examined to see whether in action they will generate unwanted consequences for other parts of a program or for the organization as a whole. This cannot be decided merely by examining the terms of an agreement. The consequences for public opinion, access to clientele, personnel selection, and the establishment of precedents and entrenched organizational machinery must be studied. This entails, in effect, considering *the power implications of co-operation,* not necessarily for the sake of power as such, but because the development and implementation of policy requires it.

These illustrations bear on the distinction between routine and critical experience, as well as on the corollary difference between static and dynamic adaptation. Routine experience works out the detailed applications of established canons. Sometimes virtually everything about an organization can be routine, including the formulation of general rules, if there is little leeway for self-definition and policies are derived automatically from precedent, authority, or technical considerations. That is why, for the bare continuity of organizational existence, leadership is often dispensable. But where leadership is required, as in the examples cited, the problem is always *to choose key values and to create a social structure that embodies them.*[21] The task of building values into social structure is not necessarily consistent, especially in early stages, with rules of administration based on economic premises. Only after key choices have been made and related policies firmly established can criteria of efficient administration play a significant role. Even then, the smooth-running machine must accept disturbance when critical problems of adaptation and change arise.

These examples suggest dynamic rather than static adaptation. The latter embraces changes that do not affect the central (self-defining) aims or methods of the enterprise. But such aims or methods are precisely what may be at stake in selective recruitment, the inculcation of core attitudes, the representation of interests, and administrative co-operation. Any of these processes may take place unconsciously, or at least outside of the attention of policy-

[21] This may be compared with individual moral experience, wherein the individual existentially "chooses" self-defining values and strives to make himself an authentic representative of them, that is, to hold them genuinely rather than superficially.

makers, so that consequences for organization character may be unanticipated and uncontrolled. Indeed, it might be useful to reserve the idea of dynamic vs. static adaptation for unconscious organizational adjustments, preserving more closely the analogy to similar processes in psychology.

The Functions of Institutional Leadership

We have argued that policy and administration are interdependent in the special sense that certain areas of organizational activity are peculiarly sensitive to policy matters. Because these areas exist, creative men are needed —more in some circumstances than in others—who know how to transform a neutral body of men into a committed polity. These men are called leaders; their profession is politics.

A political orientation is greatly needed if we are to reach a proper understanding of institutional leadership. But this orientation should not be too narrowly identified with the struggle for power. The link between "polity" and "politics" must constantly be kept in mind. To be sure, the political process always involves an actual or potential contest of wills, but it also includes the continuous redefinition of public interest and the embodiment of those definitions in key institutions. The German term *Politik*, as distinguished from *Verwaltung*, nonpolitical administration, has some of these connotations. *Politik* is not so much concerned with technical efficiency as with decisions that are open and potentially controversial. While at any given moment there may be consensus, this does not signify indifference. *Verwaltung*, on the other hand, does deal with areas of indifference. Some matters (*Politik*) are part of critical experience because they affect the way the group's character is formed, whereas other matters (*Verwaltung*) are constant despite changes in character. The existence of a contest of wills is prima facie evidence (though not conclusive) that political issues in this sense have been raised. This holds for all organizations that have freedom of self-definition, not just for public agencies.

Leadership sets goals, but in doing so takes account of the conditions that have already determined what the organization can do and to some extent what it must do. Leadership creates and molds an organization embodying—in thought and feeling and habit—the value premises of policy. Leadership reconciles internal strivings and environmental pressures, paying close attention to the way adaptive behavior brings about changes in organizational character. When an organization lacks leadership, these tasks are inadequately fulfilled, however expert the flow of paper and however smooth the channels of communication and command. And this fulfillment requires a continuous scrutiny of how the changing social structure affects the evolution of policy.

The relation of leadership to organizational character may be more closely explored if we examine some of the key tasks leaders are called on to perform:

1. *The definition of institutional mission and role.* The setting of goals is a creative task. It entails a self-assessment to discover the true commitments of the organization, as set by effective internal and external demands. The failure to set aims in the light of these commitments is a major source of irresponsibility in leadership.

2. *The institutional embodiment of purpose.* The task of

leadership is not only to make policy but to build it into the organization's social structure. This, too, is a creative task. It means shaping the "character" of the organization, sensitizing it to ways of thinking and responding, so that increased reliability in the execution and elaboration of policy will be achieved according to its spirit as well as its letter.

3. *The defense of institutional integrity.* The leadership of any polity fails when it concentrates on sheer survival: institutional survival, properly understood, is a matter of maintaining values and distinctive identity. This is at once one of the most important and least understood functions of leadership. This area (like that of defining institutional mission) is a place where the intuitively knowledgeable leader and the administrative analyst often part company, because the latter has no tools to deal with it. The fallacy of combining agencies on the basis of "logical" association of functions is a characteristic result of the failure to take account of institutional integrity.

4. *The ordering of internal conflict.* Internal interest-groups form naturally in large-scale organizations, since the total enterprise is in one sense a polity composed of a number of sub-organizations. The struggle among competing interests always has a high claim on the attention of leadership. This is so because the direction of the enterprise as a whole may be seriously influenced by changes in the internal balance of power. In exercising control, leadership has a dual task. It must win the consent of constituent units, in order to maximize voluntary co-operation, and therefore must permit emergent interest blocs a wide degree of rep-

resentation. At the same time, in order to hold the helm, it must see that a balance of power appropriate to the fulfillment of key commitments will be maintained.

In the chapters to follow, we shall consider the first three of these leadership tasks, with some passing attention to the fourth.

THREE

The Definition of Mission
and Role

We may suppose that to govern is always something of a strain; yet it is surely less demanding to preside over an organization that largely runs itself than to be confronted with the question: What shall we *do?* What shall we *be?* These questions are hard enough in matters of personal guidance; they can be enormously complicated when the character and direction of a polity is at stake.

The institutional leader in his role as goal-setter must confront all of the classic questions that have plagued the study of human aspiration. When is an aim, such as "happiness," specific enough to be meaningful? What is the right role of reason, and of opportunism, in the choice of ends? How may immediate practical goals be joined to ultimate values?

Purpose and Commitment

The aims of large organizations are often very broad. A certain vagueness must be accepted because it is difficult to foresee whether more specific goals will be realistic or wise.[1] This situation presents the leader with one of his most difficult but indispensable tasks. *He must specify and recast the general aims of his organization so as to adapt them, without serious corruption, to the requirements of institutional survival.* This is what we mean by the definition of institutional mission and role.

The term "mission" has a distinctly military flavor, but its meaning is not entirely clear even in that sphere. Emphasis is often placed on the element of *precision* in military assignments of mission. One student of administration has drawn directly on the military analogy in making the point that "a clear statement of purpose universally understood is the outstanding guarantee of effective administration."

On this point military administration taught us a real lesson. With minor exceptions, no activity was initiated by the military without clear definition, a definition cast in terms of purpose, timing, and resources; no organizational unit was set up without a statement of its mission. The success or failure of any man or of any venture was measured against this specific statement of objectives and methods. In administration, God helps those ad-

---

[1] See pp. 5–22, on the distinction between "organization" and "institution" and on the open-endedness of institutional experience. With that discussion in mind, it should be clear that this analysis does not bear on all goal-setting. Here we are dealing with the institutional definition of mission in the sense that this represents an adaptive structuring of aims that cannot be predetermined on a technological basis. Thus the assignment of combat missions becomes increasingly predeterminable as we descend the military echelons. This holds roughly for other enterprises as well.

ministrators who have a clearly defined mission, and thus the beginnings of authority commensurate with their responsibility.[2]

There is surely some undue optimism here, particularly as to the effectiveness with which the missions of high-echelon or noncombat military agencies were specified. Even at lower levels, where no great amount of experience with the type of unit established existed, the use of the word "mission" may have added an aura of clarity that was not justified on closer analysis.

While emphasizing precision and clarity, Gulick also pointed out, however, that administrative failures occurred when there was "no adequate definition of mission *in realistic terms, related to the other activities of the government.*"[3] It appears, indeed, that something more than mere precision is required. Some kind of assessment is necessary before the required clarity can be achieved. And this assessment may itself demand a period of actual experience during which the capabilities of the organization and the pressures of its environment may be tested. If this is so, then *prior* definition of mission—"no organizational unit was set up without a statement of its mission"—is not an indispensable step in organizational planning and, indeed, may result in undue rigidities if prematurely attempted. Our concern here is to emphasize that self-assessment.

In defining the mission of the organization, leaders must take account of (1) *the internal state of the polity:* the strivings, inhibitions, and competences that exist within the organization; and (2) *the external expectations* that de-

[2] Luther Gulick, *Administrative Reflections from World War II*, University of Alabama Press, 1948, p. 77.
[3] *Ibid.* Italics supplied.

termine what must be sought or achieved if the institution is to survive. Let us briefly examine each of these phases.

1. *Internal commitments.* The need to set goals with an eye to the capabilities of the organization and to the irrepressible demands of forces within it, is a problem set for the leadership of any polity, from a great nation, or combination of nations, to the smallest self-sustaining organization.

In international affairs, this problem arose in connection with the definition of "war aims" under conditions of coalition warfare. During World War II, there was much discussion of this issue, particularly among those concerned with the political implications of military operations.[4] It was felt in some quarters that "victory" was too general a term, inadequate to guide the host of decisions, both military and political, that attended the war effort. The plea was for a definition of mission, a statement of aims that would include the wider, nonmilitary (often moral) objectives of the allied powers. Those who stressed these alleged commitments—to democratic forms of government, national self-determination, etc.—were attempting to shape present goals by asserting the claims of an institutional "self" or identity.

The leaders of the joint war effort resisted this attempt to bind their hands. Winston Churchill was especially sensitive to the danger of *premature* self-definition. He did not want to limit the maneuverability of the coalition save for real advantages. He understood that the boundary between apparent and truly binding moral commitments is very fluid; and he undoubtedly recognized as a tactical device the claim of the opposition to hold views that merely

---

[4] See Hans Speier, *Social Order and Risks of War* (New York: Stewart, 1952), Chap. 29.

reflected the established policy of the community. Commitments to a solidly crystallized public opinion can be very real indeed; but opinions may also be weakly held and readily altered. It is a task of leadership to assess the extent to which even widely held views represent the polity's true self-defining commitments.

In 1940 Churchill insisted against challengers in Parliament that victory was his war aim; and the following year he said: "I have, as the House knows, hitherto consistently deprecated the formulation of peace aims or war aims—however you put it—by His Majesty's Government, at this stage. I deprecate it at this time, when the end of the war is not in sight, when the conflict sways to and fro with alternating fortunes and when conditions and associations at the end of the war are unforeseeable. But a Joint Declaration by Great Britain and the United States is an event of a totally different nature." [5] In resisting the formulation of specific war aims, Churchill was recognizing that changing events might create new obligations and opportunities that would materially affect those aims. At the same time, he accepted the need to do whatever was necessary to establish and maintain an Anglo-American coalition.

"The nature of this war, determined, as it is, by German aggression; the nature of the coalition which Germany has mobilized against herself for a second time in a generation; the respective national contributions to the defeat of Germany by the forces allied against her—all these factors have gone into the making of our war aims." [6] In this passage Speier sums up the argument of his essay, that war

[5] *Ibid.*, quoted on p. 389.
[6] *Ibid.*, p. 395.

aims could not be defined freely on the basis of abstract criteria as to what would be desirable or even effective as propaganda. Such aims were inescapably conditioned by the nature of the warring powers themselves, that is, the commitments they brought with them into the alliance. A leadership that did not undertake this self-assessment, and overlooked these limitations, would open the way to irresponsible adventurism and utopian sentimentality.[7]

Defining the aims of a coalition of sovereign states is of course exceptionally difficult, but it is the same as the basic problem in more familiar organizations. A wise leader faces up to the character of his organization, although he may do so only as a prelude to designing a strategy that will alter it. At the same time, following Churchill, he does not accept restraints unless they are truly conditions of effective action. A university president may have to accept some unwelcome aspects of alumni influence; he would be a poor leader if he did so without knowing whether this dependency was truly part of the institution's character. So too, in foreign affairs, much may be lost by an easy assumption that an American administration "cannot" support

[7] On adventurism, see *ibid.*, p. 388: "It certainly would have been folly to base a decision on their advice, for the political perspective of propagandists is exceedingly short. As experts in political warfare they would not have taken account of the traditions of our foreign policy in the Far East, the lasting interests of this country, the political relations, both at that time and after the defeat of Japan, between Britain and the United States, China and the United States, Russia and the United States. In short, the data and the considerations on which they would have based their advice would have been grotesquely inadequate in view of the great political issues that were affected by the declaration. Statesmen, not propagandists, must make policy." The mark of the statesman, we may add, is his capacity to adapt his aims to the commitments of the polity he leads, that is, to take account of the indirect and long-run consequences of current action for the evolving character of the community or enterprise.

programs abroad that are inconsistent with economic doctrines held by dominant groups at home.

The relation between purpose and institutional commitment is also revealed in the struggle over the missions of the armed services. Here the underlying problem has to do with the capacity of an agency to protect itself against inroads from organizational rivals, not merely in the short-run struggle for funds, but especially in the competition for long-run status. The institutional leaders of the various armed services recognize that the way the mission of the service is formulated will reflect, and in part influence, the evolving balance of forces.

They themselves are under strong pressure to promote definitions of mission which have the best chance of enlarging the scope, or at least protecting the flanks, of their organizations. Hence, in formulating aims and jurisdictions, the statement of mission must be more than "clear"; it must take account of the pressures that will arise from within the agency to redefine its aims in ways that lend it increased security.

For example, an independent Air Force may naturally overvalue strategic rather than tactical weapons, methods, and intelligence, particularly in an early period of intense struggle for an assured status. An emphasis on strategic competence—that is, the ability to mount an offensive using weapons that will directly and independently affect the outcome of the battle—is congenial in the struggle for autonomy and prestige. The ground forces might seek control of tactical air units, but would not readily challenge the autonomy of a strategic air command and its squadrons.

Further, an emphasis on strategic competence justifies large independent staff agencies for planning, procurement, and training, as well as for research and development. And probably most important of all, such a stress connotes, to the Air Force leaders and to the public, a sense of power that cannot so easily come from a role that emphasizes tactical air support for land armies.[8] Similar considerations apply, of course, to other agencies. Organizational design is unrealistic when it fails to take account of such tendencies.

2. *External pressures.* In addition to internal concerns, "institutional commitments" also include such externally set goals as must be accepted if significant deprivations are to be avoided. These commitments arise wherever a specific "payoff" is externally demanded and can be enforced. An effective and self-conscious leader learns to test his environment, including the strength of higher authority and the seriousness of its demands, in order to discover just what the required payoff is. As every such leader knows intuitively, to find out what one is "really responsible for" requires an assessment of the needs and responsibilities of those who formally tell him what to do.

Leadership in the United States military establishment has been confronted with this problem in an acute form. It must accurately assess the demands that are made upon it, i.e., discover its true commitments. Under modern con-

---

[8] See James A. Huston, "Tactical Use of Air Power in World War II: The Army Experience," *Military Affairs*, XIV, No. 4 (Winter, 1950), p. 172, where the following statement by former Assistant Secretary of War John J. McCloy is quoted: "It is my firm belief that the Air Forces are not interested in this type of work, think it unsound, and are very much concerned lest it result in control of Air units by ground forces. Their interest, enthusiasm and energy is directed to different fields." The conditions that channel "interest, enthusiasm and energy" are closely related to institutional development and character-formation.

ditions, these cannot be reduced to the responsibility of preparing the defense of the U.S. against the eventuality of total war. American military power may also be called upon to act in limited and peripheral controversies. Consequently, planning in the military establishment must distinguish the preparation of deterrents to the initiation of a general conflict from the development of capabilities to intervene effectively in isolable conflicts. Acceptance of an institutional commitment to be prepared for limited warfare requires much more than verbal acquiescence. Those who design weapons systems, integrated with political and economic strategy, may have to recognize, for example, that limited warfare presumes relatively inefficient operation of military forces, because an isolated conflict necessarily means that "privileged sanctuaries" exist on both sides. A commitment is not truly accepted and understood unless its consequences are also understood.

An organization's "true commitments," however, are not unchanging. They must be reassessed continuously. An air arm struggling for recognition may have, as a corollary of its weakness, no effective external demand to satisfy beyond demonstrating the utility of its weapons. This will leave it free to concentrate overwhelming attention on the building and protection of an air force. But once it assumes a central role in the defense system, it loses this freedom, and its leadership will fail if this transition is not recognized. This may be compared with the "irresponsibility" of a minority political party which, when it wins a majority and forms a government, must accept the commitments of power and forsake its narrow role of opposition.

This problem of accommodating internal and external

demands is a source of much misunderstanding. It divides administrative analysts and responsible officials into hostile camps. The leader, sensitive to internal pressures and to the heavy price that must be paid for co-operation, is impatient with the analyst whose narrow logic of efficiency leads to proposals for change that are irresponsible from the standpoint of the institution. The analyst, for his part, is sensitive to the tendency of a leader to lapse into opportunism, to conceive his entire role as one of self-defense. For the present, it appears that the analyst bears the greater fault, since his theories of organization do not adequately account for the factors with which the responsible institutional leader must deal. Even where the importance of internal morale is recognized, this tends to be restricted to a concern for the well-being and adjustment of individuals rather than of interest-groups within the enterprise and of the latter as a whole.

The Retreat to Technology

A characteristic threat to the integration of purpose and commitment—hence to the adequate definition of institutional mission—is an excessive or premature technological orientation. This posture is marked by a concentration on ways and means. The ends of action are taken for granted, viewed as essentially unproblematic "givens" in organization-building and decision-making. The enterprise is conceived of as a tool whose goals are set externally. This may not raise difficulties, if tasks are narrowly and sharply defined, as in the case of a typist pool or machine records unit. At this extreme, the organization is totally absorbed in routine tasks and leadership is dispensable. However, as we move to areas where self-determination becomes increasingly important—where "initiative" must be exercised—the setting of goals loses its innocence. In particular, if a leadership acts as if it had no creative role in the formulation of ends, when in fact the situation demands such a role, it will fail, leaving a history of uncontrolled, opportunistic adaptation behind it.[9]

The retreat to technology is associated with the difficulty of integrating political and military strategy. When military commanders—or diplomats—attempt to define a sphere of "purely military" decisions,[10] this is congenial to the creation of secure boundaries within which known principles can be applied; and it abets the avoidance of responsibility

[9] In his study of the adult education program in Los Angeles, Clark found that the leaders of the program tended to abandon a creative role in setting goals. A diffuse ideology of "service" comes down to a program based upon customer preference. The adult school is conceived of as a tool whose goals are set externally, by "the public," leaving the school official only the simple technical task of "servicing the demand," whatever that may be. This opportunism may well leave the program inadequately prepared when new agencies with clearer missions invade this growing field of work. See B. R. Clark, *Adult Education in Transition: A Study of Institutional Insecurity* (Berkeley and Los Angeles: University of California Press, 1956), pp. 145 ff.

[10] Some of General Dwight D. Eisenhower's comments in *Crusade in Europe* (New York: Doubleday, 1948) are instructive. In discussing Churchill's Mediterranean Orientation, Eisenhower points to the former's "concern as a political leader for the future of the Balkans. For this concern I had great sympathy, but as a soldier I was particularly careful to exclude such considerations from my own recommendations" (p. 194). The word "soldier" as used here and in similar contexts obscures the distinction between low-echelon and high-echelon responsibilities. See also p. 80, on the decision to attack Casablanca: "As far as I can recall, this was the only instance in the war when any part of our proposed operational plans was changed by intervention of higher authority. We cheerfully accepted the decision because the governing considerations were political more than tactical, and political estimates are the function of governments not of soldiers." Note also the following comment by Dean Acheson, June 15, 1947, then Undersecretary of State, quoted in Robert Ingrim, "The Conversion to the Balance of Power," *The Review of Politics*, Vol. 14, No. 2 (April, 1952), p. 242: "In our military operations we pursued purely military objectives. The cross-channel invasion of Europe was directed solely toward the destruction of the German armies, not the occupation of territory."

for decisions that cut across these boundaries. More important, the idea that there is a division of labor—some people charged with political decisions, others with military ones—opens the way to the evasion of responsibility even within the more narrow fields. When either political or military decisions are especially difficult, dealing with vague and unpredictable elements, it is convenient to allow the decisions to be made on other grounds.

This problem is more aggravated than eased by the ritual acceptance of Clausewitz's classic apothegm: "War is a mere continuation of policy by other means." If this means that war is not an end in itself but is determined by and subordinated to political objects, we have an important emphasis leading to the ready acceptance by military commanders of political authority. But the same formula can lead to a sharp divorce of political and military areas of decision. The military commanders have, in this perspective, only to "accept" the priority of political objectives formulated by diplomats and politicians, while they themselves give all their attention to the "purely military" tools. This point of view accommodates Clausewitz to the traditional subordination of military to civilian authority in the United States—a subtle process that permits the American military planner to cite Clausewitz with approval and at the same time to neutralize his impact upon strategic planning.

This may be clarified if we take a closer look at Clausewitz:

The war of a community—of whole nations and particularly of civilized nations—always arises from a political condition and is called forth by a political motive. It is, therefore, a political act. Now if it were an act complete in itself and undisturbed, an absolute manifestation of violence, as we had to deduce it from its mere conception, it would, from the moment it was called forth by policy, step into the place of policy and, as something quite independent of it, set it aside and follow only its own laws, just as a mine, when it is going off, can no longer be guided into any other direction than that given it by previous adjustments.[11]

In other words, if military strategy were a technology, a system having its own laws, then these laws could "take over" once the political objectives were set.

This is how the thing has hitherto been regarded even in practice, whenever a lack of harmony between policy and the conduct of war has led to theoretical distinctions of this kind. But it is not so, and this idea is radically false. . . . War is, therefore, so to speak, a regular pulsation of violence, more or less vehement and consequently more or less quick in relaxing tensions and exhausting forces—in other words, more or less quickly leading to its goal. But it always lasts long enough to exert, in its course, an influence upon that goal, so that its direction can be changed in this way or that—in short, long enough to remain subject to the will of a guiding intelligence. Now if we reflect that war has its origin in a political object, we see that this first motive which called it into existence naturally remains the first and highest consideration to be regarded in its conduct. *But the political object is not on that account a despotic lawgiver: it must adapt itself to the nature of the means at its disposal and is often thereby completely changed, but it must always be the first thing to be considered. Policy, therefore, will permeate the whole action of war,* and exercise a continual in-

[11] Karl von Clausewitz, *On War* (New York: Modern Library, 1943), pp. 15–16.

fluence upon it, so far as the nature of the explosive forces in it allow.[12]

The significant idea here is the *interrelation* of political aims and military strategy, not simply the subordination of one to the other. Further:

> Now, the first, the greatest and the most decisive act of the judgment which a statesman and commander performs is that of correctly recognizing in this respect the kind of war he is undertaking, of not taking it for, or wishing to make it, something which by the nature of the circumstances it cannot be. This is, therefore, the first and most comprehensive of all strategic questions.[13]

This decision, particularly under modern conditions, is the joint responsibility of military and political planners. It is easily blurred by general aims, such as "to achieve a stable peace" or "to defend the U.S." The design and procurement of weapons, the organization of commands, the training of troops—these and many other activities of a military establishment must rest on assumptions regarding the nature of wars to be fought. If these assumptions are not made in a conscious and controlled way, they will either be made irresponsibly by whatever group is powerful at the moment, or they will not be made, and detailed decisions will remain unguided by long-run objectives. In either case, there is a failure of institutional leadership.

The problem of politico-military integration is set by the close interdependence of means and ends. The unfolding

12 *Ibid.*, p. 16. Italics supplied.
13 *Ibid.*, p. 18.

of military power necessarily conditions political decisions regarding the use of that power. If the development of capabilities is not adequately controlled—and this will occur if purely military criteria are applied in the preparedness effort—then ends will be subordinated to means, for alternative strategies will be limited by available capabilities. This is only avoided by an integration achieved in depth, that is, when political considerations reach down to influence every important area of military planning—the design of weapons, the selection of targets, intelligence, training, etc. In effect, a new institution requiring a unified political and military leadership has arisen—the *security establishment*. The real problem of unification today is the creation of an organization that will strengthen this emerging institution and provide it with effective leadership.

The retreat to technology occurs whenever a group evades its real commitments by paring its responsibilities, withdrawing behind a cover of technological isolation from situations that generate anxiety.[14] This endangers the central task of goal-setting, particularly when there is need to accommodate a technical "logic" to political conditions and aims.

This withdrawal from institutional responsibility finds comfort in a positivist theory of administration.[15] A radical separation of fact and value—too often identified·with the

[14] The bureaucratic penchant for expansion of responsibilities (and concomitant power) is often noted. But self-restriction also occurs, often with equally serious consequences. As in the case of personalities, we have a number of characteristic responses to threat. Just as we would like to know more about the conditions under which individuals resort to one or another of such responses (aggression, withdrawal, etc.), so should this be a goal in the study of organizations.
[15] See Herbert A. Simon, *Administrative Behavior* (New York: Macmillan, 1947), pp. 45 ff.

logical distinction between fact *statements* and preference *statements*—encourages the divorce of means and ends. On this view, values belong to an alien realm, outside the pale of scientific assessment:

> No knowledge of administrative techniques, then, can relieve the administrator from the task of moral choice—choice as to organization goals and methods and choice as to his treatment of the other human beings in his organization. His code of ethics is as significant a part of his equipment as an administrator as is his knowledge of administrative behavior, and no amount of study of the "science" of administration will provide him with that code.[16]

This statement illustrates a characteristic strategy. The importance of values is affirmed, but the choice of goals and of character-defining methods is banished from the science of administration. "This emphasis on the factual does not mean that we discount the importance of values. It simply reflects our belief that the competent practitioner reaches his desired ends—whatever they may be—through a mastery of the phenomena he is dealing with and a clear, objective understanding of their behavior."[17] In other words, they say given your ends, whatever they may be, the study of administration will help you to achieve them. We offer you tools. Into the foundations of your choices we shall not inquire, for that would make us moralists rather than scientists. This recalls the separation of military and political decisions discussed above. There, too, the importance of

---

[16] H. A. Simon, D. W. Smithburg, and V. A. Thompson, *Public Administration* (New York: Knopf, 1950), p. 24.
[17] *Ibid.*, p. 20.

political ends could be affirmed while relegating them to a separate and inaccessible realm.

The difficulty in this position is not that it lacks ultimate philosophical justification. As so often happens, it is the polemical formulation that has the most impact. Like other forms of positivism, this position in administrative theory raises too bright a halo over linguistic purity. Pressing a complex world into easy dichotomies, it induces a *premature* abandonment of wide areas of experience to the world of the aesthetic, the metaphysical, the moral. Let us grant the premise that there is an *ultimately* irreducible nonrational (responsive) element in valuation, inaccessible to scientific appraisal. This cannot justify the judgment in a particular case that the anticipated irreducible element has actually been reached.

That there are wide areas of administration—as of military decision—that have a technical autonomy cannot be denied. But the real problem is: Shall this be *assumed* or is it open to investigation at every point? The effective leader continuously explores the specialized activities for which he is responsible to see whether the aims taken for granted are consistent with the evolving mission of the enterprise as a whole. The propagandist and the military commander are technicians. Each must take specific goals as given, if his technical skill is to be applied. But the institutional leader cannot permit any partial viewpoint to dominate decisions regarding the enterprise as a whole. This is well understood. Less obvious, however, is that this control will not be possible unless a true conception of the nature of the enterprise—its long-run aims as shaped by long-run commitments —is grasped and held. Leadership fails if it permits a retreat to the short run. And this retreat is facilitated by an uncontrolled reliance on technologies, for they overstress means and neglect ends.[18]

To summarize: Institutional aims cannot be taken as given, for they are conditioned by changing self-definitions, by alterations in the internal and external commitments of the enterprise. If the effect of this process is to be controlled rather than left to opportunistic adaptation, an awareness of it is essential. And we have maintained that an excessive or premature technological orientation inhibits this awareness.

Organization Roles

In the U.S. military establishment it has become common to speak of the "roles and missions" of the various armed services. This usage rests on an important insight. The mission of an organization cannot be adequately defined without also determining (a) its basic methods, the main tools or ways of acting with which it should be identified, and (b) its place among organizations that carry on related activities. These are key elements of an organization's role, and when set they go a long way toward fixing the limits within which a mission can be defined.

The idea of "role" has stimulated much interest among students of personality and social structure. Put rather generally, *a role is a way of behaving associated with a defined position in a social system.* Every society, and every group within society, assigns positions to members. These positions

[18] For a related point of view see Norton E. Long, "Public Policy and Administration: The Goals of Rationality and Responsibility," *Public Administration Review,* 14:22–31 (Winter, 1954); also Dwight Waldo, *The Study of Public Administration* (New York: Doubleday, 1955), Chap. 6.

carry expectations regarding the behavior of those who fill them. We learn how to be sons, teachers, clerks, neighbors, citizens. Some of these roles are accepted consciously and formally, others unconsciously and responsively; some are peripheral, others central to our self-conceptions. Especially relevant here is that role-*taking* connotes an adaptive process, a mode of unconscious self-structuring. It is this significance of role-taking—as against the formal and external assignment of roles—that can help us here.

These informal, emergent roles are reasonably familiar on the level of individual behavior. As we observe a group of men in conference, for example, we may note that one is a "spark plug" or "idea man" who assumes responsibility for initiating discussions; another may be the perennial arbitrator, stepping in with a soothing formula or a compromise when dissension endangers the unity of the group; still another may act as the representative of some outside interest. These roles are often independent of formally assigned positions or tasks, and are likely to be closely related to the personality structure of the individuals involved. Thus the characteristic ways of behaving are often adaptive, not consciously controlled. On the other hand, although this is rare, a group may be designed with a view to creating an optimum combination of just such roles.

Role-taking is in effect a decision by the individual—not always consciously arrived at—regarding how he ought to work. And this involves an estimate of his own place among others, including the demands made upon him and his own capabilities. This self-assessment searches out the demands and limitations which determine what means may be used, hence also the free choice of ends. A man comes to understand the roles he can play as he tests the alternatives open to him, given his own personality and the social system of which he is a part. Of course, as his place in the system changes—or as he moves to a new system—a reassessment of commitments is in order. It is probable that confusion regarding role behavior, due to inadequate self-assessment, is a major source of personal difficulty. The same logic appears to hold in organizational experience.

In his history of the Air Transport Command, Oliver La Farge points to the differing self-conceptions of the Air Service Command and the Ferrying Command:

> Air Service Command was a sort of Air Force Quartermaster and Ordnance Corps; handling supplies, maintenance, and repairs peculiar to the Air Forces. Each of the overseas Air Forces contained its own Air Service Command, of which the central, domestic organization was the parent. Understandably, A.S.C. was inclined to give heed particularly to the requests of its overseas opposite numbers. The Ferrying Command, on the other hand, would often have a different appreciation of relative urgencies, and might well substitute for some of the cargoes flown to its departure points by A.S.C. for rush delivery, others, received by mail, and requested by other agencies—including supplies needed for the maintenance of its own activities. The result was haphazard and inefficient.

> It is my own impression, fairly well grounded, I think, that A.S.C. tended strongly to the view that the Air Forces' air transportation was intended primarily for Air Force use, while increasingly *as the Ferrying Command developed its philosophy and realized its own potentialities, it moved away from this concept towards the concept of itself as an agency for the service of the whole war effort.* These differences of philosophy had historical cause: from the very beginning the Ferrying Command

served international clients in its ferrying, and its pre-war transport lines were for the use of much higher levels of government than just the Air Corps. Air Service Command's history was just the opposite.[19]

References to an organization's "philosophy," as above, very often signify that a particular way of perceiving itself has evolved. If this were not an adaptive product, reflecting an intuitive assessment of potentialities and commitments, there would be no point in such phraseology. It would suffice to indicate the formal goals and methods as prescribed by higher authority. Of course, such a philosophy, if well-established, can become accepted and even formalized in due course. Before that time, this self-conception is treated as a unique characteristic of the agency, to be learned only in close association with it. It is especially important to note the consequences for decision-making, in this case affecting the assignment of priorities to shipments.

Administrative history is replete with similar illustrations of developing organizational roles. Cline points out that as combat operations were increasingly mounted from overseas rather than from the U.S., as skill in the readying and transportation of troops and materiel developed, and as the overseas headquarters staff grew in importance, the Operations Division acted "as monitor much more often than agent of the execution of the Chief of Staff's decisions as to Army operations."[20] This shift in role reflected the chang-

[19] Oliver La Farge, *The Eagle in the Egg* (Boston: Houghton, Mifflin, 1949), p. 56. Italics supplied.

[20] Ray S. Cline, *Washington Command Post: The Operations Division* (Washington, D.C.: Office of the Chief of Military History, 1951), p. 210. It is interesting that the index (p. 411) refers to this as the "mature monitoring role" of the OPD's Theater Group.

ing capabilities of other organization units and the need for OPD to adapt itself to the changes. Millett's study of the Army Service Forces inevitably deals with the ASF's struggle to work out a role vis-à-vis the Army Ground Forces and the Army Air Forces, an effort conditioned by the ASF's own internal diversity, the basic drive of the AAF to become a separate service, and the often obscure connections between strategy and supply.[21]

An agency's general *purpose* may be to promote improved soil conservation practices, but its *role* will depend on whether it decides to do this by educational means alone, or by more aggressive methods, such as offering direct aid and establishing local "districts" with powers of control. The New Deal "action" agencies in the Department of Agriculture adopted a different role in their relation to farmers and farm organizations than had been acceptable to older agencies, and this role was intimately related to the missions that the new agencies could formulate and pursue.

Among educators today a problem of organizational role arises from the growing diversity of institutions of higher education. The public junior colleges seem to face this problem in an acute way. The junior college originally offered the first two years of college work, and viewed itself as having a preparatory function junior to the university and the four-year college. An evolution away from that accepted role seems to have gone through two stages: first, an emphasis upon terminal two-year programs as the particularly unique activity of the junior college, and secondly, the more recent tendency to define the school as a "community"

[21] John D. Millett, *The Organization and Role of the Army Service Forces* (Washington, D.C.: Office of the Chief of Military History, 1954).

college, with responsibilities for adult education as well as preparatory and terminal curricula. Whatever the reasons for this trend, it is evident that the working out of an institutional role will require an assessment of the junior colleges' own potentialities and a testing of related institutions. The relative weakness of adult education agencies undoubtedly offers the junior college administrators an opportunity to move into that area.[22]

An institutional role cannot be won merely by wishing for it or by verbalizing it clearly. It must be founded in the realistic ability of the organization to do the job. The distinctive competence of the enterprise is the vital factor. In this connection the relation between the Army Service Forces and G-4 of the War Department General Staff in World War II is revealing. The reorganization of the War Department in 1942 contemplated that G-4 would be the chief supply planning agency and that ASF would work out detailed programs and plans. But according to Millett, "In practice the 'top supply planner' of the War Department was not the Assistant Chief of Staff, G-4, but the commanding general of the Army Service Forces."[23]

This division of theory and practice had a very practical basis:

OPD [Operations Division] consistently agreed in principle that G-4 ought to establish Army-wide supply policies that would correlate logistic activities throughout the three major commands [ASF, AGF, AAF] and the overseas theaters. In practice the handful of officers in G-4 Division could offer comparatively little assistance to the mammoth Services of Supply [ASF] organiza-

[22] See Clark, *op cit.*, pp. 130 ff.
[23] Millett, *op. cit.*, p. 138.

tion or to the well-staffed OPD sections. Consequently G-4 tended to be squeezed out of an important part in logistic problems. Services of Supply proceeded to make its own policies in the course of performing day-to-day tasks delegated to it, and OPD often predetermined logistic policy by the nature of the demands it made in the interests of supporting specific combat operations.[24]

In effect, the ASF headquarters went far to displace G-4, which was then reduced to a weak and highly anomalous position in the General Staff. Whatever the formal provisions, the 1942 reorganization left G-4 without the strength to enforce the ASF's theoretical subordination to G-4's broad policy-making role. The ASF's leader, General Brehon Somervell, came to speak with increased authority as the war progressed. This was not so much the result of the formal powers of his office; rather, it emerged as the dependence of others upon the capabilities of his organization became increasingly clear.

Thus roles are shaped by capability, including the extent to which one organization is dependent upon another and must heed (or may ignore) the pressures it exerts. This is sufficiently obvious when roles are *assigned* in the course of routinely establishing well-defined organizations. A task is set forth and, as a matter of course, the key methods of working are also indicated, as is the relation of the new group to other parts of the larger enterprise. Insofar as possible, mission and role are prescribed in advance. When this can be done, institutional leadership is of little significance and technical skill can determine the selection of

[24] Cline, *op. cit.*, pp. 114 ff.

personnel. When, however, we must rely on "experience" to help define the nature of an agency, the working out of roles becomes important. Leadership—in the sense of a hand at the helm to steer a course through uncharted waters—is then *required*.

FOUR

The Institutional Embodiment of Purpose

Beyond the definition of mission and role lies the task of building purpose into the social structure of the enterprise, or, to repeat a phrase used earlier, of transforming a neutral body of men into a committed polity. In this way, policy attains depth. Rooted in and adapted to the daily experiences of living persons, policy is saved from attenuation and distortion as lines of communication are extended.

The phases of leadership as here conceived add up to a total, indivisible responsibility. There is thus no sharp division between the tasks of defining mission and embodying purpose. Each entails a self-assessment, an appreciation of internal pressures and external demands. This self-knowledge leads to the formulation of truly guiding aims and methods. It identifies opportunities as well as limitations, indicating how far leadership can or must go in changing the nature and direction of the organization. A leader will just as surely fail if he too readily yields to the limitations of his organization as if he ignores those limits. The problem is always to explore and test apparent restrictions, to see which must be accepted as inevitable, as areas of true recalcitrance, and which may be so altered as to create the institutional conditions for achieving the goals retained.

Policy and Social Structure

When we discuss large communities and great issues, there is ready agreement that policy is closely dependent on sustaining social conditions. There will be quick assent to the proposition that a democratic constitution is strong or weak according to the culture and social organization upon which it rests. A strong constitutional system is built into the underlying social structure. The latter includes the balance of power among contending interests as well as the values transmitted by family and school. But when we leave this broad arena, the basic principle that policy needs social support is easily lost.

Perhaps the difficulty of making the transition from society as a whole to smaller entities stems from our inadequate understanding of the elements of social structure. In the larger society, these elements attain gross and obvious form; but the internal social structure of specialized groupings is often hidden, or cast into unfamiliar forms, or overshadowed by the normal emphasis on avowed aims. It may be helpful, therefore, to review briefly some of those aspects of social structure that affect the maintenance and change of policy decisions.

1. *Assigned roles.* The division of labor, with its multi-

plication of more or less fixed positions, is perhaps the most obvious way of connecting policy and social structure. The assignment of formal roles sets out the tasks, powers, and expected procedures of the participants, including the lines of communication among them, according to some officially approved pattern.This is the technical organization, the rationally designed instrument, the legal system. It is not the only source of order within the group or enterprise or society, but it can often be the most important.

According to the theory developed in previous chapters, leadership declines in importance as the formal structure approaches complete determination of behavior. Management engineering is then fully adequate to the task. On the other hand, it should not be supposed that the formal system is always readily observed and understood. The officially approved patterns are not necessarily codified or even written down, nor are they always fully comprehended by the participants. There may or may not be an organization chart. Sometimes the official relations are so simple and well understood that there is no need to write them down. Or the relations may be so complex that a chart of the whole system would be too complicated to be helpful. And most important, many patterns receive official approval (or are denied it) only when they are challenged and must be submitted to the controlling officials for review. This is a problem with which lawyers are familiar, for they know how difficult it is to determine what is the law. As in the case of the law, the question is what patterns will be openly recognized and enforced as part of official policy. In any complex organization, to find this out is itself no simple task.

An assigned position or role may carry inherent difficulties that endanger the aims of policy. A classic case is that of the foreman in many industrial situations. His job requires that he represent management's interest; on the other hand, if he is to do that job effectively, he must somehow establish rapport with the men he supervises, who form their own groups and have their own interests. It is difficult to do both of these things at once, yet both are required. As a result, there is a built-in tension in the foreman's role, a tension that probably is inherent in any role that combines the exercise of authority with a need for face-to-face, empathic communication. Therefore, organizational design, even when dealing with apparently simple aspects of the division of labor, must be based on an accurate understanding of the social structure created in the course of assigning formal roles.

2. *Internal interest-groups.* Interest-groups take many forms within large organizations. They range from the small informal group of workers seeking protection from potentially arbitrary rules to the large department able to summon its own loyalties. Some such groups will be weak, others strong. Some will muster support only from within the enterprise, others will find external allies. Some interest-groups follow the lines of the formal structure, transforming technical units into unities of persons; others cut across the officially approved lines of communication. But from the standpoint of the leader all have this basic significance: *they represent sources of energy,* self-stimulated, not wholly controllable by official authority. They may subvert the enterprise or lend it life and strength. It is the task of leadership, in embodying purpose, to fit the aims of the organization to the spontaneous

interests of the groups within it, and conversely to bind parochial group egotism to larger loyalties and aspirations. There are a number of important ways in which interest-groups may serve the ends of policy. The most obvious is the defense of a value by an organization unit that is psychologically as well as formally committed to it. If we inspect any large organization, we soon discover that at least some of its constituent units are the guardians of particular standards or aims. The personnel department defends standards of employee selection and training; accounting has its commitments to standards of reporting and fiscal control; sales defends lines of communication to buyers; production is committed to a schedule of output. All of these units are expected to defend the values entrusted to them. Top management has the authority (and may have the power) ultimately to dispose of the resulting conflicts; but it must have confidence that each constituent unit is maximizing the potentialities and defending the integrity of its special province. The transformation of technical units into interest-groups, largely through personal identification, strengthens these commitments.[1]

Thus particular values or policies find a *social base* in the group structure of the enterprise. But more general policy also needs a social base, a source of more than formal support, a center from which influence may radiate, a training ground for loyal and self-conscious adherents. Where leadership undertakes the task of truly directing the organization into desired channels, it must search for internal

---

[1] The general problem of internal interest-groups in administration is well treated in H. A. Simon, D. W. Smithburg, and V. A. Thompson, *Public Administration* (New York: Knopf, 1950).

sources of political support. This may take the form of creating new groups committed to new policies; or of using existing constituent units to serve as such a base. This strategy attempts to order the interest structure of the enterprise—especially the relative power of contending factions—and thus to control the conditions that affect the evolution and viability of policy.

3. *Social stratification.* The usual administrative organization includes a system of ranking. This has many uses, including fixing authority, dividing the work effectively, and supplementing formal incentives. The effects of such a system go beyond these technical functions, however. The life experiences of men at different levels in the organization differ, and these variations affect (1) how individuals in similar social positions view the world and themselves, and (2) the stake they have in the enterprise. As the ranking system shapes the general social behavior of the men who hold the ranks, social stratification emerges.

Organizations are both aided and hindered by this transformation of technical rankings into social strata. On the one hand, the development of appropriate attitudes lends support to the hierarchical system: men who have feelings of deference toward their superiors will more readily accept commands. On the other hand, the generation of special interests and attitudes by the status system brings rigidities into the organization and tends to break the unity of the enterprise.

Many of the problems created by social stratification are readily handled at the level of human relations diagnosis and treatment. Thus we know that communication among organization members is filtered as it moves up and down the line. Unpleasant information is withheld from superiors; subordinates frequently misinterpret offhand comments by their chiefs. Problems of misunderstanding and false perception, insofar as they spring from interpersonal relations, may be dealt with by management engineers who have learned their social psychology. Such problems arise continuously in any organization and do not necessarily require the attention of leadership, at least after sensitivity to human relations has been built into the organization's methods of supervision.

On the other hand, the gap between higher and lower levels in the enterprise may go beyond individual dissatisfaction or misunderstanding, to raise *political* questions affecting the basic distribution of power. For this reason, the problems of trade-union power cannot be handled by routine management *expertise* until after the fundamental issues of recognition and prerogative are settled, if they ever are.

4. *Beliefs.* The social structure of an organization also includes the relevant shared beliefs of the participants. It obviously matters a great deal whether management is perceived as benevolent or hostile. Belief systems may arise internally, as products of social stratification and the formation of interest-groups. They also reflect the social backgrounds of the personnel, who may have brought distinctive outlooks with them when recruited. As in any polity, the existence of set beliefs creates problems for the leader who undertakes to move in new directions.

A leader must know how to use law to neutralize belief by splitting it from behavior; and to employ law as a creative agency restructuring environments to foster desired understandings. The effort of the military to abandon racial segregation has involved both of these techniques. When this problem arises in administration, assuming secure control by the directing group, we see a blending of the human relations and political perspectives. The ultimate aim is political, and some of the devices (e.g., use of law) are political, but much may also be done by changing the conditions that influence interpersonal experience.

It is characteristic of authoritarian situations that political problems become readily transformed into administrative ones. Thus public opinion within the administrative organization tends to be viewed as something to be handled from the top, as a problem of organization design, training, and selective recruitment. However, political problems persist as long as conflict over policy can express itself through subordinate leaders who are too strong to be handled by administrative fiat. Only when such potential opposition has been leveled and the possibilities of its arising anew foreclosed, do we approach the pure type of authoritarian system. So long as that state has not been reached—and this is scarcely the case even in military organizations—leaders are faced with the need to assess the political capabilities of those holding undesired views, particularly whether they can form effective power blocs within the enterprise. It is often necessary to adapt the technical organization to this aspect of the social structure in order to redistribute or isolate recalcitrant elements. At the same time, this "pluralism" may be perceived as a constructive source of creative effort and a secure leadership may allow it considerable free rein.

5. *Participation.* The social structure of an organization is not mapped until we understand the different kinds and

degrees of commitment that members have to the enterprise. "Membership" does not mean the same thing to all who belong to an organization. Thus individuals differ widely in the importance they assign to their own membership and to the organization itself. It will often (but not always) be found that leaders place a higher value on the organization than do nonleaders. Since the former usually have a greater personal investment in the organization, this is hardly surprising. Morale is closely related to the possibility of increasing participation as a way of developing personal commitment to the organization. The difficulty is, however, that the division of labor usually provides but few opportunities for significant participation by the members.

Participation also affects communication. Members playing different roles, and involved in varying degrees, will differ in their ability to understand the reasons behind many decisions. Many members will have only partial views of the organization, and only a limited understanding of its objectives and principles. And because of weak or narrowly defined participation, their experience within the organization may offer little opportunity for greater comprehension. This makes it difficult to channel information easily, and especially, to hold the organization to its basic goals and values. Many organizations discover that they must adapt communication to the varying social situations of the participants. They also find that under conditions of low participation it is necessary to multiply controls, always guarding against misunderstanding of information and directives. The connection between participation and communication is of central importance in contemporary studies of organizational effectiveness.

In addition to its effect on personal stake or commitment, and on communication, differential participation affects the distribution of power within the organization. This is perhaps most evident in voluntary associations, where the highly restricted participation of members often amounts to virtual abdication; or, on the other hand, greater involvement may sustain internal political factions.

In administrative organizations participation also affects the distribution of power in a number of ways. Varying degrees of interest may affect the willingness of even high officials to expend the energy necessary to influence decisions. Some staff members may actually represent outside interests, and this will be the most significant meaning of their participation. And there may be important unintended effects on the power structure when efforts are made to increase participation of subordinates as a way of improving morale or communication; the groups set up may not be content to continue as mere devices of management.

6. *Dependency.* An executive may become the prisoner of a staff group on which he is dependent for information and specialized skills. Or the "staff" organization may be relatively weaker than the "line" because members of the staff units are dependent on the line officials for success in their day-to-day work as well as in their careers. Similarly, the dependence of rank-and-file members on the special capabilities of experienced leaders is an important basis for the tendency to self-perpetuation of leaders in many voluntary associations.

These situations suggest the value of understanding who needs whom. Of course, much of this is explicitly set out in the assignment of formal roles, which is why "reorganization" is often fraught with both terror and opportunity. Dependency patterns are also *indirect* products of the division of labor. The technical allocation of positions carries with it special opportunities for access to communication, for direct contribution to the most vital work of the enterprise, for personal advancement, for contact with outside groups. These opportunities affect the dependence of different parts of the organization on the goodwill of other parts as well as their relative ability to influence the evolution of policy. This phenomenon has received little explicit attention in the study of social structure.

*　　*　　*

These six elements of social structure, taken together, form a complex network of relations among persons and groups. This network acts as a filter through which policy is communicated; and it represents a system of accommodation among potentially conflicting parts. As a result, policy may be nullified in the filtering process; and any imbalance may lead to active measures for self-protection or aggrandizement by constituent units. To become the master of his organization, the leader must know how to deal with the social structure in all its dimensions.

When we say that policy is built into the social structure of an organization, we mean that official aims and methods are *spontaneously protected or advanced*. The aspirations of individuals and groups are so stimulated and controlled, and so ordered in their mutual relations, as to produce the desired balance of forces. This is, of course, the explicit aim of formal role assignment, but that assignment is inadequate by itself to fulfill the aim. In order to provide support for a policy, it may be necessary to alter the social structure. This occurs when "new blood" is brought in and made effective by changes in old lines of communication and dependency. Or it may be concluded that in the given circumstances the policy is not a viable one. In either case, a clear picture of the social structure of the enterprise, as a basis for making essentially political decisions, will be required.

The relation between social structure and policy may be approached in a piecemeal way, to discover the specific institutional conditions that support specific policies. For instance, certain patterns of belief and perception are suitable to an aggressive propaganda policy; others tend to nullify it. This may help us in the design of recruitment and training procedures, as well as in deciding what kinds of tasks may be brought together in the same agency. Or, to take an even more difficult problem, we may attempt to discover a pattern of participation by agency representatives on coordinating committees and staffs that will mitigate the tendency of such representatives merely to defend the interests of their agencies. The comparative study of similar problems in varying situations would undoubtedly lead to results of practical value.

In the long run, however, effective diagnosis depends on the discovery of general relations between types of policy orientation and kinds of social support. In other words, are there any clues to the *chararacteristic* troubles that arise in typical situations? This assumes that organizations do find themselves in "typical situations" and that these situations impose more or less uniform limitations upon the policymaker, or offer him characteristic opportunities.

A Historical Perspective

In the search for more general connections between policy and social structure, something may be gained from the study of organization histories. Thus, in a review of group studies in social psychology, Daniel Katz called attention to some of the characteristics of organizations that may be associated with growth patterns:

What is still very much needed for social psychology in general, as well as for a knowledge of leadership, is a set of descriptive concepts for the attributes of organizations which will go well beyond the old formal-informal distinction. For example, we need to direct attention to such elementary aspects of organizations as growth patterns. A rapidly developing organization which has certain goals to achieve under emergency time-pressures presents an entirely different time pattern from a stable organization which may have passed the peak of its power. In the former case, the leadership pattern may emphasize initiative, creativity, daring and, to some extent, a rejection of traditional pathways to goals and even a reformulation of organizational goals. The organization may be one in which there is tremendous upward mobility and high motivation. In the latter case of the older, even declining, institution, the pattern may be one of conformity to tradition, an emphasis upon conventional pathways to conventional goals and even a change from the goal of the organization to the goal of efficiency as such. It is only necessary to maintain motivation at a minimum and efforts are bent toward stability rather than toward maximum productivity.[2]

[2] Daniel Katz, "Social Psychology and Group Processes" in C. P. Stone and D. W. Taylor (eds.), *Annual Review of Psychology*, Vol. II (Stanford, Calif.: Annual Reviews, Inc., 1951), p. 144.

These remarks suggest the need to place the interpretation of organizational behavior in historical perspective. Apparently similar events or practices should not be compared directly, but only as their relation to the organization's stage of development is determined. The design of forms and procedures will then be guided by this interpretation. Administrative issues will be decided only after a diagnosis that takes account of the historical context.

The language of evolution or life-cycle can be misleading when applied to organizations, but at least a natural-history approach can call attention to the developmental problems that arise in organizational experience. In doing this, we must distinguish problems posed by the task at hand, which do not call for organizational changes, from problems that are set for an organization by the stage of growth in which it finds itself. Some of these are quite obvious, as when we anticipate the need for more regularized budgeting procedures as size increases. Less obvious are problems that emerge as changes occur in the roles and needs of the participants and of the organization as a whole. Although such changes may be consciously planned and directed, they are characteristically unplanned and responsive. Taken as a total experience, each such history is of course unique. Nevertheless, to the extent that similar situations summon like responses from similar groups, we may expect to find organizational evolutionary patterns. The hope is that this uniformity, once discovered, may provide tools for more adequate description and more perceptive diagnosis.

Certain types of problems seem to characterize phases of an organization's life-history. As these problems emerge, the organization is confronted with critical policy decisions. Examples of these developmental problems are:

1. *The selection of a social base.* Among the critical decisions facing leadership, closely related to the definition of mission, is the selection of a clientele, market, target, allies, or other segment of the environment to which operations will be oriented. Personnel recruitment, public relations, and many other areas of decision will be affected by this key choice of an external "social base." The early phase of an institution's life is marked by a scrutiny of its own capabilities, and of its environment, to discover where its resources are and on whom it is dependent. The achievement of stability is influenced by this appraisal; and the future evolution of the institution is largely conditioned by the commitments generated in this basic decision. Of course, the "decision" is not always consciously made; and often the outcome is forced upon the organization by compelling circumstances which leave little freedom of choice.

When a merchant adapts his enterprise to a particular market, say for luxury goods; when a political organization bases itself on some special social force, say the labor movement or business interests; when a government agency adapts itself to the influential groups it must please in order to stay alive—there is created an effective and controlling environment of decision. As these commitments evolve, the organization loses its purity as an abstractly or ideally envisioned entity; it assumes a definite role in a living community; it becomes institutionalized. The *design* of that role, insofar as freedom to do so exists, is very largely a matter of choosing the social base upon which the organization will rest. Often this outcome is not designed but simply emerges in an unplanned way, as a precipitant of many short-run decisions.

2. *Building the institutional core.* Another developmental problem is that of creating an initial homogeneous staff. The members of this core group reflect the basic policies of the organization in their own outlooks. They can, when matured in this role, perform the essential task of indoctrinating newcomers along desired lines. They can provide some assurance that decision-making will conform, in spirit as well as letter, to policies that may have to be formulated abstractly or vaguely. The development of derivative policies and detailed applications of general rules will thus be guided by a shared general perspective. This is especially important, of course, where the assessment of tasks and results cannot be settled by routine formulae. As always, the "openness" of decision-making calls for leadership, in this case to build a social structure that will induce a spontaneous regularity of response. Where this regularity may be imposed formally, as a clear-cut technical matter, leadership is more readily dispensable.

The creation of an institutional core is partly a matter of selective recruiting, and to this extent overlaps with the task of selecting a social base. By choosing key personnel from a particular social group, the earlier conditioning of the individuals can become a valuable resource for the new organization. Conversely, of course, just such conditioning is in question when a particular source of personnel is *rejected*. But core-building involves more than selective recruiting. Indoctrination and the sharing of key experiences

—especially internal conflicts and other crises—will help to create a unified group and give the organization a special identity.

The importance of core-building for institutional development is quite familiar. The recruitment of key personnel for the new CIO Steel Workers Organizing Committee from the United Mine Workers Union decisively influenced the later evolution of the steelworkers' union, particularly in ensuring tight control from the top; the dependence of the new "action agencies" in the U.S. Department of Agriculture on a pool of agricultural personnel brought up in another tradition required special emphasis on "orientation," i.e., self-definition, in the new agencies; the emergence of communism from a socialist background entailed a very large effort to overcome earlier conditioning and create a new institutional core. Even in business, where self-definition may seem less important than in political and other community enterprises, there is a need to build a self-conscious group that fully understands "the kind of company this is."

While core-formation may be a conscious and designed process, it also develops naturally, as an indirect result of day-to-day interaction. Hence the general problem of leadership is *control* of core-formation, whether to build one congenial to desired policy or to restrain one that creates unwanted rigidities in organization and policy. This problem is developmental. It is associated with a special phase in the organization's life-history, and must be dealt with in some way if control over the long-run evolution of policy is to be maintained.

3. *Formalization.* A very familiar phase in the life-history of organizations is the formalization of procedure. The or-

ganization reduces its dependence on the personal attributes of the participants by making supervision more routine and by externalizing discipline and incentive. Formalization limits the open-endedness of organizations and thereby reduces the number of leadership decisions required.

While this process is well known, it is worth noting here that the transition from personal supervision to managerial control is developmental and brings with it characteristic growing pains, including shifts in top personnel. Formalization should be understood as an emergent problem, for in diagnosis we must ask whether a given instance of formalization is *premature,* as well as whether necessary adaptations to the new stage have been made. Premature formalization, sometimes reflecting an overemphasis on the quick achievement of clarity in communication and command channels, may seal off leadership during the early stages of organization building, when it is most needed. As a result, leadership decisions—such as those affecting the institutional core and the social base—may be left to uncontrolled adaptation.

A historical sensitivity will aid the planner to revamp organizational structure in the light of developmental changes that have created new risks and opportunities. These advantages will be illustrated in the following comments on (1) some characteristic personnel crises in organizational evolution, and (2) the relation of decentralization to social integration.

Personnel Crises and Growth Stages

Developmental changes are most sharply reflected in personnel turnover. This does not mean just any turnover, such as routine attrition and replacement, but that involving a shift from one type of person to another. As new problems emerge, individuals whose ways of thinking and responding served the organization well in an early stage may be ill-fitted for the new tasks. Characteristically, this is not so much a matter of technical knowledge as of attitudes and habits. These shape an individual's outlook and orientation to the job, resulting in a distinctive pattern of emphasis and judgment. The more firmly set the personal pattern—a condition that may be highly desirable during creative periods of organization development—the less adaptable is the individual.

A good example of personnel crisis associated with developmental change is found in the early history of many unions and in particular of the United Automobile Workers. This union was founded in 1935, in a situation of severe economic distress. Militance was the keynote during its early years. The problem of leadership was largely one of conducting a struggle for power and recognition, in which techniques of mobilization necessarily played a large role. The men who came to the fore reflected this emphasis on militancy. Successful office-seekers in the locals were those who could be counted on to deal roughly with management. Such men met the needs of a union more concerned with hewing out a place for itself, and surviving, than with responsible management of a stable organization.

After the union achieved its initial aims, the older methods of direct strike action, associated with a class-struggle outlook, became inappropriate and sometimes even harmful. Work stoppages were costly for both labor and management. While they might be thought indispensable as demonstrations of power by a group struggling for recognition, they could not be satisfactory as a permanent way of dealing with management. As this became clear, new leadership—locally and nationally—was indicated. While earlier shop stewards and local presidents were chosen for their strength in facing up to management, now it was necessary to choose men at the local level who could keep out of trouble and avoid unnecessary shutdowns. There began a movement away from militance, toward more astute negotiating techniques. To implement this change, a widespread turnover of personnel was required.[3]

Similar problems arise in industrial management. A characteristic crisis is the shift from a production orientation to an emphasis on sales and public relations. The Ford Motor Company, among others in the auto industry, went through a crisis of this sort. The organization that produced the famous "Model T" was dedicated to the goal of producing more cars per day at an ever lower cost per car. In this it was highly successful. But the organization that made this achievement possible failed to recognize or respond to changes in the market. Consumer preference was shifting to comfort, styling, and performance. By 1926, when sales were off disastrously, Ford permitted his company to engage in a national advertising campaign. He accepted this technique grudgingly, only under the pressure of a major crisis.

But much more than advertising was needed to permit sales an adequate role in the organization. Design and engineering had to be influenced as well. Finally, in 1927, production of the Model T was stopped, and Ford undertook

---

[3] Based on an unpublished analysis by Edward Boehm. For the experience in the steel industry, see Clinton S. Golden and Harold J. Ruttenberg, *Dynamics of Industrial Democracy* (New York: Harper, 1942), pp. 59 ff.

the monumental task of retooling for a completely new automobile and rebuilding factory interiors so that it could be manufactured. It was now clear that the very techniques that brought about the great production achievement of the Model T were stumbling blocks when the need was speedy and efficient changeover. Huge, single-purpose machines had been built into production lines where more flexible machines were needed to keep up with periodic model changes. When the policy that "the customer could have any color he wanted as long as it was black" gave way to color styling, the old finishing process became completely obsolete. "Nearly every piece of the company's monolithic equipment, laid out on the assumption that the Model T would linger on forever, had to be torn down and rebuilt. The staggering changeover necessitated the replacement of some 15,000 machine tools, the total rebuilding of another 25,000, as well as the redesigning and rearrangement of $5,000,000 worth of dies and fixtures." [4]

Conversion to the Model A took eighteen months and cost $100,000,000. Yet even this did not bring about the changes in orientation, with attendant upward revisions in the status of sales and public relations activities, that were required. Only after World War II was a reorganization in depth completed. The Ford enterprise paid a heavy price for a policy, valuable in the early state of development, that was not abandoned in good time. Given a deep initial commitment, so often required by pioneering ventures, such adaptations are likely to require correspondingly severe shifts in personnel.

[4] Keith Sward, *The Legend of Henry Ford* (New York: Rinehart, 1948), p. 199.

An important caution is necessary at this point. Such terms as "early" and "late" can be misleading, if they are taken too literally, as referring to chronological periods in a *given* organization. In fact, of course, we must see an organization in its historical context, as an institution. When, for example, the production problems of an industry have been largely solved, it is not to be expected that a new firm will go through a stage of "production orientation." It begins at the level already reached by the industry (or branch of it) as a whole. This means that developmental analysis is most relevant where there is "openness," where the organization enters new paths. Every organization does this to some extent, and has some developmental problems, but it is safe to say that these problems will be most acute among ground-breaking enterprises or where there are few sure guides to decision and action.

It seems evident that the proper assignment of personnel and the diagnosis of administrative troubles will gain from a better understanding of the relation between personnel orientations and organization life-history. Consider, for example, the following administrative problem: In the case of a large research organization, what sort of men should be chosen as chiefs of the various research divisions? Should they be subject-matter specialists or administrators? This decision presumes an assessment of the stage of development in which the organization finds itself. If basic policy has not been worked out or not yet effectively communicated, if key staff members have not been chosen, there may well be a need for the research-oriented, creative person, whose job will be to give direction to the division and to build that orientation into its personnel structure and operating procedures. When these tasks have been accomplished, it may be in order for a person whose speciality is administrative skill to take over the reins. The selection of key personnel requires an understanding of the shift in problems that occurs as the organization moves from one stage of development to another. And for best results the participants should be able to recognize the phase through which they are passing.

The connection between personnel crisis and developmental stages recalls the suggestive images used by Machiavelli and Pareto to designate leadership types. In the latter's discussion of the "circulation of elites" we are offered the hypothesis that innovator types (the "Foxes") are needed to devise new programs and techniques. To be effective, these "Foxes" must be associated with more conservative, forceful elements having strong institutional loyalties and perseverance. As the new system or institution gains strength, and has something to defend, the "Foxes" become more expendable; and the "Lions" take over complete control, trimming innovations to meet the needs of survival. But this in turn may limit adaptation to new conditions. The institutional problem is to keep a proper balance of the social types needed at each stage. This theory might well be salvaged and reformulated in more workaday terms for use in the study of specific institutions, including administrative structures, rather than of whole societies and historical epochs.

Decentralization and Social Integration

In the design of decision-making procedures, much attention is devoted to the maintenance of policy without overly concentrated or multiplied controls. Various patterns of administrative decentralization have been developed to achieve this balance. Here too, however, diagnosis and prescription should heed the life-cycle conditions that affect the application of administrative principles. Precepts regarding the value of administrative decentralization will be more adequately formulated and more intelligently applied if they take account of organizational evolution.

The need for centralization declines as the homogeneity of personnel increases. A unified outlook, binding all levels of administration, will permit decentralization without damage to policy. When top leadership cannot depend on adherence to its viewpoint, formal controls are required, if only to take measures that will increase homogeneity. On the other hand, when the premises of official policy are well understood and widely accepted, centralization is more readily dispensable. Hence we shall expect that a relatively high degree of centralization will be required in the early stages of institutional development. Later, when homogeneity has been achieved, decentralization will be feasible without undue loss of control.

A study of administrative behavior in the U.S. Forest Service showed how this informal control could be substituted for more formal centralization:

But to interpret dispersal of structure and function as the absence of central control would be to fly in the face of the facts. For what is to be said, then, of an organization which carefully instills in the minds of its members an identity of outlook, a sameness of objectives, a sense of mutual obligation and of common identification and common values? It is clear that the organization would enjoy a unity, indeed, almost a conformity, of action as marked as that of any group in which the members must take all matters to a central point for decision. There would be as noticeable an absence of internal conflict as in any organization in which all possibly controversial matters are settled in a single office. In a word, though one type of organization may manipulate the thinking and values of its members while the other directly controls their behavior by orders, both types succeed in obtaining the kind of administrative decisions and behavior they desire; one just as certainly as the other molds the actions of its members. It is meaningful, therefore, to call one centralized and the other decentralized only in the sense that they utilize different techniques to secure identical results.[5]

Of course, "identical" is not meant literally, since the social integration envisioned may well yield more flexible and efficient types of decision-making. (It may also result in excessive conformity and rigidity.) The point is simply that conformity and thus control may be won through other than formal devices. And a certain amount of social homogeneity is required if subordinate personnel are to be allowed wide discretion in the application of policies to special circumstances.

Decentralization requires a preparatory period of training, in which leadership has the opportunity to influence deeply the ideas that guide decision-making at lower levels. This influence may take the form of indoctrination, including the informal promotion of an official philosophy or even formal schooling. Educational measures are especially important where circumstances impose barriers to close contact. More useful is the collaborative development of plans and policies by as many levels of the organization as possible,

[5] Herbert Kaufman, "Field Man in Administration" (Unpublished doctoral dissertation, Columbia University, 1950), pp. 225 f.

so that a unified view, or at least understanding of the controlling viewpoint, will be achieved. This entails the participation of top leadership in low-echelon decisions and the participation of subordinate staff personnel in high-level planning.

If the chief aim of this participation is understood—the creation of a unified staff—then these procedures may later be changed, in the direction of greater clarity of responsibility and command, without excessive strain. The normal process will be one of withdrawal of top leadership from decision-making delegated to lower echelons, and a lessening of participation by subordinate personnel in policy planning. Once the task of unification is accomplished—to the extent required by the nature of the enterprise—the narrower techniques of administrative management can be brought into play. In particular, extensive delegation of responsibility may be worked out on the assumption that the prerequisite social organization is in being.

Perhaps the best-known example of decentralization in American industry is found in General Motors.[6] Yet historically the period of decentralization was preceded by a decade of tight control. Centralization was required in order to reorient the organization after the DuPont interests took over the company. The significance of this experience for administrative analysis is (1) that decentralization would have been an unfeasible policy during the stage of reorientation; and (2) that the period of tight control probably created precisely those social conditions essential to a later policy of decentralization.

Participation is a way of deepening communication and

[6] See Peter F. Drucker, *Concept of the Corporation* (New York: John Day, 1946), pp. 41 ff.

developing group cohesion. (This is sometimes associated with democratic doctrine, but need not be so understood.) Yet a given level of communication and cohesion may be adequate to the circumstances at hand. Hence maximal participation is not always required. It should be prescribed only when there is a problem of cohesion, when cohesion cannot be taken for granted and must be reinforced. Among the general conditions generating such problems is the newness of organizations. We expect, therefore, that leadership will attend to the problem of cohesion before techniques of administration that presume its solution are instituted. At least it will be understood that this problem must be solved before the full promise of these administrative methods can be fulfilled.

An interesting example of progressively lessening need for centralized co-ordination has been observed in the California prison system.[7] In that system there are Reception-Guidance centers which have the responsibility, based on "treatment" principles, for designating the particular prison to which the inmate should be assigned. This procedure runs up against another problem of the system as a whole, the need to have some reasonable balance of populations within the prisons. It was felt in the beginning that the Guidance Center personnel should not have the task of adapting their treatment-based assignment decisions to the demands of operating the system; that they should concentrate strictly on the inmate and his needs, letting other officials worry about adjusting the recommendations. A headquarters job was created—the Supervisor of Classifica-

[7] As reported in unpublished notes by Sheldon L. Messinger, who is currently engaged on an institutional study of the California Department of Corrections.

tion and Parole—with the responsibility of adjusting transfer recommendations to system demands. The device also reflected the policy of putting in charge of the Guidance Center a professional treatment specialist who would not, at least in the early period, be familiar with the operation of the prison system. There was also the wish to keep whoever did the adjusting close to headquarters, so that he could be constantly apprised of changes in the population needs of the prisons.

The continued need for this type of headquarters co-ordination is now questioned, however. Certain basic policies are now more widely disseminated and accepted. The need to have professionally self-conscious clinical personnel as heads of the Guidance Centers is less urgently felt, because the clinical program is now well established and no longer requires aggressive defense. The two Guidance Center chiefs can now be (and are) primarily administrators. Moreover, the present heads have in the past held subordinate professional posts in the Guidance Centers and have also served in the headquarters Bureau of Classification. Finally, the technique of population balancing is generally known and is no longer experienced as a threat by the professional personnel. All this leads to the feeling that the work of the Supervisor of Classification has become more routine and less important.

A high administrator of the system said in 1954:

"In general, I feel that the position of Associate Warden, Reception-Guidance Center [head of the Guidance Center] should be strengthened administratively to eliminate the present situation of being a 'middle man.' By this, I mean that he is currently forced by administrative rules to be an apologist for his staff when their recommendations, which he presumably has endorsed, are rejected or changed by the representatives of the Director's staff and conversely, to his own staff when rationalizing for them the rejection of recommendations which he has presumably approved. I feel that administratively the dividing of this responsibility for review of the output of the Reception-Guidance Centers is a serious administrative defect. . . . Further, it must be pointed out that both Associate Wardens formerly worked as representatives of the Bureau of Classification and therefore are quite aware of transfer policy and the technique for equalizing and meeting institutional population quotas." [8]

If this administrative procedure is defective, it is so not as an abstractly incorrect rule of administration but because it is inappropriate to the new stage of institutional development.

Thus a historical (perhaps even an evolutionary) perspective can tell us something about the conditions under which such administrative methods as decentralization may be applied. The lesson is that in appraising organizations we cannot draw conclusions regarding administrative practices unless we can place those practices in a developmental context. As we learn more about the social conditions that characterize various growth stages, we should be able to formulate principles capable of guiding the application of general precepts to specific situations.

In concluding this section, it may be well to recall the orientation that prompted an emphasis on organizational evolution. First, we have been interested in exploring the *natural* processes that condition organizational experience. Hence a concern for the products of adaptive, responsive

[8] Quoted *ibid.*

behavior, among which are social homogeneity and cohesion. Second, we are examining the area of *critical* experience, which calls for leadership rather than routine management. The study of growth stages, especially as they bear on the restructuring of role and need, seems to cast some light on critical phases. Third, the developmental patterns noted here have a common element in that they reflect changes in *commitment,* in those relations to men and ideas that are not readily altered. Changes in commitment—to markets or clienteles, to constituencies, to allies, to an institutional core, to ingrained habits of thought and modes of response—create organizational crises. The resolution of these crises markedly affects the range of competence of the enterprise as well as the survival of its distinctive aims and methods.

Precarious Values and the Defense of Integrity

Although every effective policy requires sustaining social conditions, the urgency of this need varies greatly. It is most important when aims are not well defined, when external direction is not easily imposed or easily maintained, when fluid situations require constant adaptation, and when goals or values are vulnerable to corruption. This open-endedness, we have argued earlier, generates the key problems of institutional leadership. Among these is the defense of institutional integrity—the persistence of an organization's distinctive values, competence, and role.

The integrity of an institution may be threatened, regardless of its own inner strength, if sufficiently great force is applied to it. But in diagnosis we are mainly concerned with points of special inner weakness. From that standpoint we may say that institutional integrity is characteristically vulnerable *when values are tenuous or insecure.* This variation in the strength of values has received little scientific attention.[9] Yet it commands much energy and concern in practical experience. In the course of building an organization, and establishing its separate units, group responsibility is fixed. But these "custodians of policy" will not be equally capable of sustaining their distinctive aims and standards. We need to know something about the social conditions that affect this competence.

The ability to sustain integrity is dependent on a number of general conditions, including the adequacy with which goals have been defined. Here we shall consider a special problem, the relation between precarious values and professional or elite autonomy. Our primary aim is to illustrate the potential contribution of institutional analysis to administrative theory. Therefore it may be helpful if, before dealing with administration proper, we first consider some other applications of the general idea. To do this, let us examine three ideas and how they are related.

Elite. For present purposes, this term refers to any group that is responsible for the protection of a social value. Often this responsibility is accepted consciously, but that is not essential. There would be no great harm in substituting the term "profession" or "professional group" for "elite," so long as the definition is kept in mind. Both terms have been used to designate men who carry out this basic social function.

[9] For an attempt to specify the meaning of "precarious values," based on the orientation developed here, see B. R. Clark, "Organizational Adaptation and Precarious Values," *American Sociological Review,* Vol. 21, No. 3 (June, 1956), pp. 328 f.

Social values are objects of desire that are capable of sustaining group identity. This includes any set of goals or standards that can form the basis of shared perspectives and group feeling.

Autonomy is a condition of independence sufficient to permit a group to work out and maintain a distinctive identity.

These definitions are hardly final or unambiguous, but they will permit us to make some progress. The basic relation to be considered may be formulated as follows: *The maintenance of social values depends on the autonomy of elites.* Let us turn to the bearing of this proposition on (1) the general problem of institutional integrity, as it is familiar to the historian of culture; (2) certain aspects of political organization, as revealed in the history of Communism; and (3) certain technical problems of administrative management.

1. *Elite autonomy and cultural viability.* In modern society, social institutions are exposed to many demands to provide short-run benefits for large numbers. Educational and political agencies have been sharply affected by this process, and they tend to adapt themselves to the mass by permitting participation on the basis of low standards of knowledge and conduct. This adaptation makes it increasingly difficult for professional groups or elites to maintain their own standards, hence ultimately their special identity and function. And they tend to lose their "exclusiveness"—that insulation from day-to-day pressures which permits new ideas and skills to mature.

It appears that what is critically necessary for the functioning of elites is enough autonomy to allow the maturation and protection of values. The achievement of this autonomy is a central task of professional associations, "little magazines," specialized schools, and a host of other devices for self-insulation used by groups in society that wish to protect and promote a particular set of values. Private universities with large endowments are better insulated from day-to-day pressures than are many public institutions, sustaining the autonomy of their professors and scientists. Literary elites are hard-pressed from the standpoint of autonomy because of the high cost of publishing and the commitment of that industry to the mass market. Hence literary groups may seek the shelter offered by private colleges able to subsidize esoteric journals. In our culture, the legal and medical professions are well insulated, others much less so. Those who are concerned for the protection of political, educational, aesthetic, and religious values, must find ways of providing the conditions needed to sustain the autonomy of culture-bearing elites.

The point summarized here is quite familiar to the historian of culture. But the basic relation between value maintenance and elite autonomy may cast some light on rather different and more unfamiliar situations.

2. *Political isolation and the combat party.* In an earlier work referred to previously, the author attempted to analyze the organizational aspects of Communist strategy and to understand the inner dynamics of the "combat" party. Here is a characteristic elite phenomenon. The Bolsheviks attempt to build a leadership corps of "professional revolutionaries" that maintains a long-run dedication to the aims of Communism while engaged in the struggle for immediate power objectives. Any elite group, to maintain itself as such, must

take special measures to protect its integrity. Among the most common of these measures are: (1) selective recruiting; (2) specialized training, as in the elite school; and (3) withdrawal from the everyday pursuits of mankind, especially from exposed competition in the marketplace. Each of these devices strengthens the isolation of the elite, its capacity to shape its own identity free of external pressures. All of these devices, among others, have played an important part in Bolshevik political and organizational experience. For the purpose of this discussion, a single illustration will suffice.[10]

An important phase of Bolshevik political history took place during a period of "ultra-left isolation" from about 1924 to 1935. During these years the Communist parties throughout the world followed a policy of extreme (but mostly verbal) aggression against democratic and socialist forces. The latter were presented as "social fascists," against whom all means, including violence, were in order. This was a period of "dual" trade-unionism, in which the Communists disdained to work within the legitimate—"yellow" —labor movement but created their own "red" trade-unions. The latter usually included only Communist party members and their periphery, but they did lay the basis for later effective penetration of the mass unions.

The general effect of this ultra-left activity was organizational isolation. At first glance, this seems to have been self-defeating, and the later reversal might be understood as a corrective measure. The Communists did indeed isolate themselves from the main body of the workers, hence from any significant influence in society. Nevertheless, *this long period of isolation served to consolidate the power of the Rus-*

[10] Selznick, *The Organizational Weapon*, pp. 126 ff.

sian party over the International, to test and train the party cadres, and to intensify reliance on conspiratorial methods. Out of this period of ultra-left phrases, revolutionary adventures, splits, purges, and intensive indoctrination, there emerged a powerful political movement. This is not to say that the Communist leaders designed it so. But the modern Communist movement is a product of its history; it owes elements of strength, as well as of weakness, to the apparently irrational period of "social fascism" and "united front from below."

Specifically, this character-forming period readied the organization for a new period of propagandistic deception and organizational maneuver. After 1935, organizational isolation was definitively—and permanently—rejected. Open Communist propaganda was increasingly retired to the background, and the party turned to slogans of "unity," "peace," and similar generalities that might offer access to wider sections of the population. The "red" unions were abandoned and the party entered the legitimate trade-unions. The old aggression against "bourgeois" politicians was relaxed, and the party could support a Franklin Roosevelt when that was expedient.

On the organizational front the new turn permitted a wide range of targets, a multiplicity of new devices and maneuvers, unrestricted by the need continuously to repeat revolutionary phraseology. It opened up a whole new arena for political intervention from which the Communists have not withdrawn despite subsequent major shifts in the party line. The Seventh Congress of the Comintern, in 1935, initiated a permanent effort to break through long-standing isolation by the free use of deceptive symbols and organizational stratagems. In effect the conclusion was drawn that the day for worrying about the Communist integrity of the parties was past; the basic weapon had been forged; the time for wielding it effectively had arrived. Insistence on correct ideological formulae was to be exchanged for acceptance of more flexible slogans, and organizational practices were to be adapted to the conditions of the arena.

The period of ultra-left propaganda and organizational isolation was an *internally-oriented* period, dedicated to preparing a weapon that would maintain its integrity when it was thrown into active political combat. It was this period of sharp break with the looser, more relaxed socialist traditions; of heavy emphasis on party discipline, on political orthodoxy, on conspiracy, and on intensive indoctrination that made possible the maintenance of the hard core of the party despite severe shifts in political line (as at the time of the Stalin-Hitler pact), and despite the heavy pressures on party members to become adapted to trade-unionist and reformist perspectives. Communist members could become *deployable agents* in other organizations—always serving the interests of the party—only as they accepted the authority of the party leadership. To create an organization able to exert such authority was a task that could not be accomplished without strenuous effort. Most of the early history of the Communist movement was devoted to that task of building "revolutionary cadres."

The Communist combat party, by assuming an ultra-left propaganda posture, preserved its autonomy as an elite, isolating itself from the pressures of the political arena *until it was ready to resist those pressures.* Put another way, the Bolsheviks wished to maintain an institution embodying a precarious value: a party competent to deploy members as disciplined agents. A period of organizational isolation, fostered by ultra-left propaganda, helped to contribute the sustaining social conditions. This only repeats, in a particular context, the generalization noted above, that the maintenance of values depends on the autonomy of elites. We have drawn here on a general institutional theory to help make sense of a particular historical development. The better developed such a general theory is, the more inferences can be drawn regarding the phenomena under analysis.

3. *Administrative autonomy and precarious values.* One of the perennial problems confronting the architect of organizations is administrative autonomy. When should an activity be thought of as distinctive enough to be allowed a relatively independent organizational existence? Should political intelligence personnel be assigned to geographic desks in the State Department, or should they have their own organization? Should education in a trade-union be bracketed administratively with public relations? Should psychological warfare operations be attached to G-2?

Applying the theory of professional or elite autonomy dicussed above, we may recast the problem in the following way:

(1) When an organizational unit is set up, especially if it is large enough to have its own administrative staff, an elite is created in the sense that some men now become professionally responsible for the protection of a social value. Probably this elite function is the source of most organizational rivalry.

(2) It follows from our general theory that isolation is necessary during periods of incubation and maturation, but

may be modified when this character-forming task has been accomplished. Moreover, the more readily subject to outside pressure a given value is, the more necessary is this isolation. (Roughly, this means that the more technical a function is, the more dispensable is organizational isolation. In highly technical fields, a large degree of *social* isolation is won simply by the use of esoteric techniques and language, and by the evident importance of professional criteria as to appropriate methods of work.)

(3) This provides us with a principle that can help in making decisions about administrative autonomy. We appraise the given value (be it intelligence, health, education, psychological warfare, or customer service) and consider (*a*) whether the elite function of value-protection is required, and (*b*) whether special safeguards against outside pressures are needed. This may lead to the conclusion, for example, that a new staff unit ought to be attached directly to a top-command echelon—not permanently, but during a period when its basic perspectives are being laid down, its distinctive mission being evolved. Or such a unit might be attached to one *quite different* in function (but institutionally strong) for the express purpose of offering a haven to an organization charged with defending and developing a precarious value. Strong groups with similar responsibilities, who might feel threatened by the new unit, would thus be restrained from attacking it too directly.

An approach to autonomy in these terms is a radical departure from the attempt to build organizations according to the logical association of functions. That principle—which will of course always be relevant—is often violated in practice, and for good reason. It must be violated whenever values are unequal in strength. Organization planning is unrealistic when it fails to take account of the differential capacity of subordinate units to defend the integrity of their functions. The theory of elite autonomy permits us to deal with this problem systematically and openly. This is important because many decisions that do in fact face up to this issue must now be justified obliquely, and be half-hidden, since there is no accepted administrative principle allowing organizations to be treated differently according to the strength of their respective values.

Let us apply this idea to the classic headquarters-field problem. Given a headquarters organization and a field organization, to whom shall subject-matter specialists (say in recreation, medicine, or personnel selection) be responsible? To the technical staff chief at headquarters or to the head of the local field organization? The dilemma is that the headquarters staff will be concerned over values (whether good accounting procedure or good medical practice), but the field executive will be under pressure to get an immediate job done while perhaps taking insufficient account of the long-run consequences of his decisions. One answer has been "dual supervision," in which certain officers are thought of as "administratively" responsible to one superior while "technically" responsible to another.[11] This recognizes the special role of technical staff personnel in developing and defending values.

But "dual supervision" really presumes an optimum situation, in which a strong value-oriented elite (the technical

[11] See A. W. MacMahon, J. D. Millett, and Gladys Ogden, *The Administration of Federal Work Relief* (Chicago: Public Administration Service, 1941), Chap. 11; also J. D. Millett, "Field Organization and Staff Supervision," *New Horizons in Public Administration,* University of Alabama Press, 1945.

staff) has had enough autonomy to lay down professional criteria that are accepted by the line officials. When, as in medicine and engineering, values have been effectively matured, dual supervision is relatively easy, for the boundaries within which the technical and administrative personnel may operate are reasonably clear-cut and are tacitly or even formally recognized as part of the code of proper behavior. Even in such fields, however, where the boundaries are unclear, as in the development of criteria for certifying military personnel fit for duty, it is to be expected that the professional group will be vulnerable to external pressure.

When we deal with *precarious* values—say an information and education program, or a political intelligence operation —special attention to the problem of elite autonomy is required. In such cases, we may accept a much closer relation between headquarters staff and field personnel than would otherwise be justified, because we recognize the need for intensive communication during character-forming periods. Such periods also require special measures to resist potentially corrupting external pressures, and this means a more intense professional self-consciousness. Suppose a government agency establishes a new labor relations policy, championed by the headquarters staff, but of necessity using line executives (say on construction jobs) who are not fully in sympathy with this policy. In the early days of the agency, we may expect a centralization of the labor relations program, perhaps manifested in a rule permitting workers to register complaints directly at headquarters and in the establishment of field labor relations specialists who conceive of themselves as self-conscious outposts of headquarters in an alien environment. This centralization permits the autonomous maturation of values; later, when the desired policies have been well established, a greater degree of decentralization will be in order.

In general, headquarters staffs perform elite functions. They tend to be highly self-conscious about the values for which they have assumed responsibility. That is why co-operation among field representatives is often easier to attain than co-operation among headquarters staffs. And it is the headquarters staff that puts pressure on its field representatives to avoid co-operation that may prejudice distinctive identity. The appropriate response to this phenomenon is neither to deplore it generally nor to accept it as inevitable, but to investigate the actual circumstances to determine how much elite autonomy is in fact needed, given the strength of the value in question.

The theory of elite autonomy, thus applied, helps make explicit what is really at stake in much confused conflict and oblique debate. It leads us away from rigid rules of administrative organization, yet it helps to identify the key elements that need to be controlled and in terms of which guiding principles can be set forth.

*   *   *

Few aspects of organization are so important, yet so badly neglected by students of the subject, as this problem of institutional integrity. No one knows how much in resources and strategic capability is sacrificed by the U.S. military establishment (and other great enterprises) as a result of organizational rivalry. The educated guesses would run very high. Yet this rivalry is no simple result of personal egotism; it is closely related to the legitimate effort of leaders to defend the values with which they have been entrusted. The military services have faced this problem continuously, and have tried at various times to define the administrative conditions of professional integrity. The Air Force fought for decades to be recognized as an agency that needed a distinctive identity in order to do its job effectively. This identity, it was held, would need support in the following "clearly demonstrated principles":

(1) Freedom through "independent experimentation and research" to develop new forms of aircraft; (2) the power to procure for itself new types of planes; (3) freedom to select and train the special personnel to operate airplanes and to plan air tactics; (4) the power to create an air staff to plan air strategy; and (5) the power to "insure the permanence of the technique" thus created through an adequate permanent force of regular officers.[12]

Similarly, during the controversy over unification, a naval leader attempted to set out an administrative principle that would help protect the integrity of the services. He called for recognition of two phases in decision-making regarding major weapons: development and procurement. In the first phase, each service should be autonomous in deciding what weapons should be carried through to the prototype stage, without veto power by other services. Decisions on large-scale procurement, however, justify a greater degree of external co-ordination and control.[13]

And here is a defense of Marine Corps aviation:

[12] John D. Millett, "The War Department in World War II," *American Political Science Review*, XL (1946), p. 870.
[13] Statement of Arthur W. Radford, Admiral, U.S. Navy, *Hearings*, U.S. House Committee on Armed Services, 81st Congress, 1st sess. (1949), p. 48.

I will probably be asked: Why a Marine aviation at all? Why can't naval aviation or Air Force squadrons support Marine landing forces? In answer, I would invite your attention to the peculiar qualifications of Marine aviators. Unique among military fliers, each Marine pilot is required to serve two years as a Marine infantry officer before he may even apply for aviation duty. Thereafter, throughout his career, he must attend the same professional schools as does his ground contemporary; he frequently finds himself a member of a combined staff where his daily work requires intimate familiarity with the tactics of all elements of the Marine Corps. In other words, he knows what the commander on the ground needs and he knows how to deliver it. What is equally important, he knows what a deployed battalion looks like from the air; the troops of that battalion have no hesitancy in asking him to drop bombs or shoot rockets in the closest proximity to their front lines.[14]

Whatever the merits of the claims and counterclaims implicit in these statements, they do indicate the practical importance of identifying the conditions that sustain the integrity of an enterprise. This applies, of course, not only to the great agencies mentioned here, but to all organizations and constituent units that are in some degree custodians of a policy. These statements also suggest that the defense of integrity is not a matter of sheer organizational survival; it is rather the policy, the mission, the special capability—in a word, the identity of the group that is at stake.

As we have suggested, the basic answer society has evolved for the protection of institutional integrity is professionalism. While some very general aspects of this phenom-

[14] Statement of General Vernon E. Megee, *ibid.*, p. 198.

enon have been known since Plato's time, very little attention has been given it as *operating within specific organizations* rather than in society at large. In the case of organizations that initiate ideas, where creativity and independence are at a premium, the role of internal and external professional associations can be crucial, buttressing the independence of key personnel. If a man is to take risks, he needs social supports. Yet the role of professionalism will vary in different types of organizations, depending on the balance required between those men whose primary commitment is to a specific organization and those whose sense of responsibility is broader. These matters are as yet hardly touched by students of the sociology of professions.

FIVE

Conclusion

The main task of this essay has been to explore the meaning of institutional leadership, in the hope of contributing to our understanding of large-scale organization. We have not offered recipes for the solution of immediate problems. Rather, we have sought to encourage reflection and self-knowledge, to provide some new guides to the diagnosis of administrative troubles, and to suggest that the posture of statesmanship may well be appropriate for many executives who now have a narrower view and a more limited aspiration.

This final chapter summarizes the main ideas developed above, with some added notes on responsibility and creativity in leadership.

Beyond Efficiency

It is easy to agree to the abstract proposition that the function of the executive is to find a happy joinder of means and ends. It is harder to take that idea seriously. There is a strong tendency not only in administrative life but in all social action to divorce means and ends by overemphasizing one or the other. The cult of efficiency in administrative theory and practice is a modern way of overstressing means and neglecting ends. This it does in two ways. First, by fixing attention on maintaining a smooth-running machine, it slights the more basic and more difficult problem of defining and safeguarding the ends of an enterprise. Second, the cult of efficiency tends to stress techniques of organization that are essentially neutral, and therefore available for any goals, rather than methods peculiarly adapted to a distinctive type of organization or stage of development.

Efficiency as an operating ideal presumes that goals are settled and that the main resources and methods for achieving them are available. The problem is then one of joining available means to known ends. This order of decision-making we have called *routine,* distinguishing it from the realm of *critical* decision. The latter, because it involves choices that affect the basic character of the enterprise, is the true province of leadership as distinct from administrative management. Such choices are of course often made unconsciously, without awareness of their larger significance, but then the enterprise evolves more or less blindly. Leadership provides guidance to minimize this blindness.

In many situations, including those most important to the ultimate well-being of the enterprise, goals may not have been defined. Moreover, even when they are defined, the necessary means may have still to be created. Creating the means is, furthermore, not a narrow technical matter; it involves molding the social character of the organization. Leadership goes beyond efficiency (1) when it sets the basic mission of the organization and (2) when it creates a social organism capable of fulfilling that mission. A company's decision to add a new product may be routine if the new is but an extension of the old. It is a critical decision, however, when it calls for a re-examination of the firm's mission and role, e.g., whether to remain primarily a producer of a raw commodity or to become a manufacturer of consumer goods. The latter choice will inevitably affect the outlook of management, the structure and control of the company, and the balance of forces in the industry.

Not only the setting of goals by top leadership but many other kinds of decisions at all administrative levels can be part of critical experience. Anything may enter the area of critical experience providing it affects the ability of the organization to uphold its distinctive aims and values. If an atmosphere congenial to creative research is required, the methods of assigning work, policing diligence, or judging output must be governed by that aim. This often produces tension between those executives most sensitive to the special needs of the enterprise and those who seek to apply more general and more neutral techniques of efficiency.

In going beyond efficiency, leadership also transcends "human engineering," at least as that is usually understood. Efficiency may require improved techniques of communication and supervision, but these techniques are largely indifferent to the aims they serve. The human relations specialist like his predecessor, the efficiency expert, is characteristically unmoved by program, by the content of what is to be done. His inspiration does not derive from the aim of creating a particular kind of auto firm or hospital or school. Rather his imagination is stirred by the processes of group interaction and the vision of a harmonious team, whatever its end may be.

This does not mean that communication and other forms of human interaction are unimportant to leadership. They do become vitally important when they are given content, when they serve the aim of fashioning a distinctive way of thinking or acting and thus help establish the human foundations for achieving a particular set of goals. Indeed, the *attainment* of efficiency, in the sense of transforming a basically inefficient organization into one that runs according to modern standards, may itself be a leadership goal. But here the task is a creative one, a matter of reshaping fundamental perspectives and relationships. It should not be confused with the routine administrative management of an organization already fully committed to the premises of rational accounting and discipline.

Beyond Organization

The design and maintenance of organizations is often a straightforward engineering proposition. When the goals of the organization are clear-cut, and when most choices can be made on the basis of known and objective technical criteria, the engineer rather than the leader is called for. His work may include human engineering in order to smooth personal relations, improve morale, or reduce absenteeism. But his problem remains one of adapting known quantities through known techniques to predetermined ends.

From the engineering perspective, the organization is made up of standardized building blocks. These elements, and the ways of putting them together, are the stock-in-trade of the organization engineer. His ultimate ideal is complete rationality, and this assumes that each member of the organization, and each constituent unit, can be made to adhere faithfully to an assigned, engineered role. Furthermore, the role assigned does not stem so much from the peculiar nature of *this* enterprise; rather, the roles are increasingly generalized and similar to parallel roles in other organizations. Only thus can the organization engineer take advantage of the growth of general knowledge concerning the conditions of efficient administrative management.

The limits of organization engineering become apparent when we must create a structure *uniquely adapted to the mission and role of the enterprise.* This adaptation goes beyond a tailored combination of uniform elements; it is an adaptation in depth, affecting the nature of the parts themselves. This is really a very familiar process, brought home to us most clearly when we recognize that certain firms or agencies are stamped by distinctive ways of making decisions or by peculiar commitments to aims, methods, or clienteles. In this way the organization as a technical instrument takes on values. As a vehicle of group integrity it becomes in some degree an end in itself. This process of becoming infused with value is part of what we mean by institutionalization. As this occurs, *organization management* becomes *institutional leadership.* The latter's main responsibility is not so much technical administrative management as the maintenance of institutional integrity.

The integrity of an enterprise goes beyond efficiency, beyond organization forms and procedures, even beyond group cohesion. Integrity combines organization and policy. It is the unity that emerges when a particular orientation becomes so firmly a part of group life that it colors and directs a wide variety of attitudes, decisions, and forms of organization, and does so at many levels of experience. The building of integrity is part of what we have called the "institutional embodiment of purpose" and its protection is a major function of leadership.

The protection of integrity is more than an aesthetic or expressive exercise, more than an attempt to preserve a comforting, familiar environment. It is a practical concern of the first importance because the defense of integrity is also a defense of the organization's *distinctive competence*. As institutionalization progresses the enterprise takes on a special character, and this means that it becomes peculiarly competent (or incompetent) to do a particular kind of work. This is especially important when much depends on the creation of an appropriate atmosphere, as in the case of efforts to hold tight transportation schedules or maintain high standards of quality. A considerable part of high-level salesmanship is an effort to show the firm's distinctive capability to produce a certain product or perform a special service. This is important in government too, where competing agencies having similar formal assignments work hard to develop and display their distinctive competencies.

The terms "institution," "organization character," and "distinctive competence" all refer to the same basic process —the transformation of an engineered, technical arrangement of building blocks into a social organism. This transition goes on unconsciously and inevitably wherever leeway for evolution and adaptation is allowed by the system of technical controls; and at least some such leeway exists in all but the most narrowly circumscribed organizations. Leadership has the job of guiding the transition from organization to institution so that the ultimate result effectively embodies desired aims and standards.

Occasionally we encounter a self-conscious attempt to create an institution. The history of the *New York Times,* for example, suggests such an effort. Ideals of objectivity and public instruction have deeply affected many aspects of the organization, including the nature of the staff, the pace of work, the relations to advertisers, and its role among other newspapers. Of course, it is relatively easy to see a newspaper as an institution because it so apparently touches familiar ideals. Whether it truly embodies those ideals is a question that appeals to all as relevant and sensible. But we have argued that the formation of institutions is a far more widespread phenomenon and is a process that must be understood if the critical experience of leadership is to be grasped.

Institutional analysis asks the question: What is the bearing of an existing or proposed procedure on the distinctive role and character of the enterprise? Very often, of course, organization practices are institutionally neutral, just as many body functions are independent of the personality structure. But the question must be put. Thus recent efforts to establish statistical and administrative control units for the judiciary look to improvements in the division of labor among judges, and to similar matters, for the achievement of a more "orderly flow of litigation." The proponents of greater efficiency reaffirm their adherence to the principle of judicial independence, and they believe this principle is not affected by improved administrative controls; they seek to "serve, not supervise." In this case it seems altogether likely that a wide measure of reform in judicial administration is possible without seriously undermining the judge's traditional image of his own role and sense of independence. Nevertheless, the experience of other institutions suggests that the managerial trend can have far-reaching effects, and the question of whether a set of proposed administrative reforms endangers the maintenance of desired values is always legitimate and necessary.

The lesson is this: Those who deal with the more obvious ideals—such as education, science, creativity, or freedom—should more fully recognize the dependence of these ideals on congenial though often mundane administrative arrangements. On the other hand, those who deal with more restricted values, such as the maintenance of a particular industrial competence, should be aware that these values too involve ideals of excellence, ideals that must be built into the social structure of the enterprise and become part of its basic character. In either case, a too ready acceptance of neutral techniques of efficiency, whatever their other merits, will contribute little to this institutional development and may even retard it.

The study of institutions is in some ways comparable to the clinical study of personality. It requires a genetic and developmental approach, an emphasis on historical origins and growth stages. There is a need to see the enterprise as a whole and to see how it is transformed as new ways of dealing with a changing environment evolve. As in the case of personality, effective diagnosis depends upon locating the special problems that go along with a particular character-structure; and we can understand character better when we see it as the product of self-preserving efforts to deal with inner impulses and external demands. In both personality and institutions "self-preservation" means more than bare organic or material survival. Self-preservation has to do with the maintenance of basic identity, with the integrity of a personal or institutional "self."

In approaching these problems, there is necessarily a close connection between clinical diagnosis of particular cases and the development of sound general knowledge. Our problem is to discover the characteristic ways in which *types* of institutions respond to *types* of circumstances. The significant classifications may well depart from common-sense distinctions among enterprises according to whether they perform economic, political, religious, or military functions. We may find that more general characteristics, such as professionalized managerial control, competence to make full use of creative talents, or dependence on volunteer personnel, are more helpful in classifying organizations and in understanding the types of problems they face and the solutions that may be available. Students of personality have had similar objectives and have made greater, although still very crude, efforts to get away from common-sense rubrics. Yet, despite theoretical difficulties, real progress has been made, and clinical success in diagnosis and therapy lends confidence to the larger scientific quest.

Responsible Leadership

As the organization becomes an institution new problems are set for the men who run it. Among these is the need for institutional responsibility, which accounts for much of what we mean by statesmanship.

From a personal standpoint, responsible leadership is a

blend of commitment, understanding, and determination. These elements bring together the selfhood of the leader and the identity of the institution. This is partly a matter of self-*conception,* for whatever his special background, and however important it may have been in the decision that gave him his office, the responsible leader in a mature institution must transcend his specialism. Self-*knowledge* becomes an understanding not only of the leader's own weaknesses and potentialities but of those qualities in the enterprise itself. And the assumption of command is a self-*summoning* process, yielding the will to know and the will to act in accordance with the requirements of institutional survival and fulfillment.

From a policy standpoint, and that is our primary concern, most of the characteristics of the responsible leader can be summarized under two headings: the avoidance of opportunism and the avoidance of utopianism.

Opportunism is the pursuit of immediate, short-run advantages in a way inadequately controlled by considerations of principle and ultimate consequence. To take advantage of opportunities is to show that one is alive, but institutions no less than persons must look to the long-run effects of present advantage. In speaking of the "long run" we have in mind not time as such but how change affects personal or institutional identity. Such effects are not usually immediately apparent, and therefore we emphasize the lapse of time. But changes in character or identity may occur quite rapidly.

Leadership is irresponsible when it fails to set goals and therefore lets the institution drift. The absence of controlling aims forces decisions to be made in response to immediate pressures. Of course, many large enterprises do drift, yet they survive. The penalties are not always swift, and very often bare survival is possible even though the fullest potentialities of the enterprise are not realized and significant changes in identity do occur.

The setting of institutional *goals* cannot be divorced from the enunciation of governing *principles*. Goal-setting, if it is institutionally meaningful, is framed in the language of character or identity, that is, it tells us what we should "do" in order to become what we want to "be." A decision to produce a new product or enter a new market, though it may set goals, is nevertheless irresponsible if it is not based on an understanding of the company's past and potential character. If the new venture, on analysis, requires a change in distinctive competence, then *that* becomes the new goal. Such a goal is bound up with principles because attaining and conserving a distinctive competence depends on an understanding of what standards are required and how to maintain them. If a grain processing firm moves into the chemical industry, it must learn how to build into its new division the competence to keep pace with rapid technological changes on pain of falling behind in the struggle against obsolescent products and techniques. Because the technique of attaining this is seldom based on explicitly formulated principles, it would be prudent to staff the new division, *especially* at the top, with men drawn from the chemical industry rather than with men drawn from the parent firm and representing its tradition and orientations.

When an enterprise is permitted to drift, making short-run, partial adaptations, the greatest danger lies in uncontrolled effects on organization character. If ultimately there is a complete change, with a new character emerging, those who formed and sustained the organization at the beginning may find that they no longer fit the organization. There is also the likelihood that character will not really be transformed: it will be *attenuated and confused.* Attenuation means that the sought-for distinctive competence becomes vague and abstract, unable to influence deeply the work of staff and operating divisions. This occurs when the formulation of institutional goals is an afterthought, a way of rationalizing activities actually resulting from opportunistic lines of decision. A confused organization character is marked by an unordered and disharmonious mixture of capabilities. The practical result is that the organization cannot perform any task effectively, and this weakens its ability to survive in the face of strong competition.

In addition to sheer drift stemming from the failure to set institutional goals, opportunism also reflects an excessive response to outside pressures. To be sure, leaders must take account of the environment, adapting to its limitations as well as to its opportunities, but we must beware of institutional surrender made in the name of organizational survival. There is a difference between a university president who *takes account* of a state legislature or strong pressure groups and one who permits these forces to determine university policy. The leader's job is to *test* the environment to find out which demands can become truly effective threats, to *change* the environment by finding allies and other sources of external support, and to *gird* his organization by creating the means and the will to withstand attacks.

Here, too, we come back to the problem of maintaining

institutional integrity. The ultimate cost of opportunistic adaptation goes beyond capitulation on specific issues. A more serious result is that outside elements may enter the organization and dominate parts of it. When this happens the organization is no longer truly independent, no longer making specific compromises as necessity dictates while retaining its unity and distinctive identity. Rather, it has given over a piece of itself to alien forces, making it possible for them to exercise broader influence on policy. The transformation of compromise or even defeat into partial organizational surrender can sometimes be a conscious measure of last resort, but it also occurs without full awareness on the part of the participants. In our study of the Tennessee Valley Authority, referred to above, just such a phenomenon was observed. A political compromise with local and national agricultural interests was implemented by permitting part of the TVA as an organization to be controlled by those forces, with extensive and unanticipated effects on the role and character of the agency. The avoidance of opportunism is not the avoidance of all compromise; it is the avoidance of compromise that undermines institutional integrity.

Opportunism also displays itself in a narrow self-centeredness, in an effort to exploit other groups for immediate, short-run advantages. If a firm offers a product or service to other firms, expectations of dependability are created, especially in the matter of continuing supply. If supplies are abruptly discontinued, activities that depended upon them will suffer. Hence a firm's reputation for dependability and concern for others becomes a matter of great importance wherever continuing relationships are envisioned. To act as if only a set of impersonal transactions were involved, with no responsibility beyond the strict terms of a contract, creates anxiety in the buyer, threatens to damage *his* reputation for dependability, and in the end weakens both parties.

The responsible leader recognizes the need for stable relations with the community of which his organization is a part, although he must test the environment to see how real that requirement is. A large and enduring enterprise will probably have to contribute to the maintenance of community stability, at least within its own field of action. In industry, this may take the form of participation in trade associations and other devices for self-regulation. The marginal firm, on the other hand, can afford to be irresponsible in dealing with the community because it is less dependent on stable relations with other firms or with a special clientele or labor force. Such firms have also less need of responsibility to themselves as institutions, for they have fewer hostages to fortune. Generally, responsibility to the enterprise and to the community go hand in hand, each increasing as the transition from organization to institution becomes more complete.

If opportunism goes too far in accepting the dictates of a "reality principle," utopianism hopes to avoid hard choices by a flight to abstractions. This too results in irresponsibility, in escape from the true functions of leadership.

In Chapter Three we outlined some of the sources of utopianism. One of these is the *overgeneralization of purpose*. Thus "to make a profit" is widely accepted as a statement of business purpose, but this is too general to permit responsible decision-making. Here again, the more marginal the business, that is, the greater its reliance upon quick returns, easy liquidation, and highly flexible tactics, the less need there is for an institutionally responsible and more specific formulation of purpose. Indeed, the very generality of the purpose is congenial to the opportunism of these groups. But when institutional continuity and identity are at stake, a definition of mission is required that will take account of the organization's distinctive character, including present and prospective capabilities, as well as the requirements of playing a desired role in a particular industrial or commercial context.

Utopian wishful-thinking enters when men who purport to be institutional leaders attempt to rely on overgeneralized purposes to guide their decisions. But when guides are unrealistic, yet decisions must be made, more realistic *but uncontrolled* criteria will somehow fill the gap. Immediate exigencies will dominate the actual choices that are made. In this way, the polarities of utopianism and opportunism involve each other.

Another manifestation of utopianism is the hope that the solution of technical problems will solve institutional problems. We have discussed the "retreat to technology" as a way of avoiding responsibility for the multiple ends that must be satisfied if the institution as a whole is to be successful. To be "just a soldier," "just an engineer," or even "just a businessman" is inconsistent with the demands of statesmanship. It is utopian and irresponsible to suppose that a narrow technical logic can be relied on by men who make decisions that, though they originate in technical problems, have larger consequences for the ultimate evolution of the enterprise and its position in the world.

This brand of utopianism is associated with adventurism, a willingness to commit the organization as a whole on the basis of a partial assessment of the situation derived from a particular technological perspective, such as that of the propagandist in foreign affairs or the engineer or designer in industry. Here again the utopian as technologist becomes the victim of opportunism.

Responsible leadership steers a course between utopianism and opportunism. Its responsibility consists in accepting the obligation of giving direction instead of merely ministering to organizational equilibrium; in adapting aspiration to the character of the organization, bearing in mind that what the organization has been will affect what it can be and do; and in transcending bare organizational survival by seeing that specialized decisions do not weaken or confuse the distinctive identity of the enterprise.

Creative Leadership

To the essentially conservative posture of the responsible leader we must add a concern for change and reconstruction. This creative role has two aspects. First, there is what we have called the "institutional embodiment of purpose." Second, creativity is exercised by strategic and tactical planning, that is, analyzing the environment to determine how best to use the existing resources and capabilities of the organization. This essay has not treated the problem of externally oriented strategies. On the other hand, what can be done to establish policy internally depends upon the changing relation between the organization and its environment.

The inbuilding of purpose is a challenge to creativity because it involves transforming men and groups from neutral, technical units into participants who have a peculiar stamp, sensitivity, and commitment. This is ultimately an educational process. It has been well said that the effective leader must know the meaning and master the techniques of the educator. As in the larger community, education is more than narrow technical training; though it does not shrink from indoctrination, it also teaches men to think for themselves. The leader as educator requires an ability to interpret the role and character of the enterprise, to perceive and develop models for thought and behavior, and to find modes of communication that will inculcate general rather than merely partial perspectives.

The main practical import of this effort is that *policy will gain spontaneous and reasoned support*. Desired ends and means are sustained and furthered, not through continuous command, but as a free expression of truly accepted principles. This presumes that at least the core participants combine loyalty to the enterprise with a sensitive awareness of the principles by which it is guided. Loyalty by itself is not enough, just as blind patriotism is insufficient. There must also be an ability to sense when a course of action threatens institutional integrity.

To be sure, this ideal of rational, free-willed consent is virtually impossible to achieve in organizations that have narrow, practical aims and whose main problem is the disciplined harnessing of human energy to achieve those aims. But such organizations, just because of this narrowness, are but meagerly institutionalized and have correspondingly little need for executive statesmanship. The creativity we speak of here is particularly necessary—and peculiarly possible—where, as discussed earlier, the transition from organization to institution is in process or has occurred.

To create an institution we rely on many techniques for infusing day-to-day behavior with long-run meaning and purpose. One of the most important of these techniques is the elaboration of socially integrating myths. These are efforts to state, in the language of uplift and idealism, what is distinctive about the aims and methods of the enterprise. Successful institutions are usually able to fill in the formula, "What we are proud of around here is. . . ." Sometimes, a fairly explicit institutional philosophy is worked out; more often, a sense of mission is communicated in more indirect but no less significant ways. The assignment of high prestige to certain activities will itself help to create a myth, especially if buttressed by occasional explicit statements. The specific ways of projecting a myth are as various as communication itself. For creative leadership, it is not the communication of a myth that counts; rather, creativity depends on having the will and the insight to see the necessity of the myth, to discover a successful formulation, and above all to create the organizational conditions that will sustain the ideals expressed.

Successful myths are never merely cynical or manipulative, even though they may be put forward self-consciously to further the chances of stability or survival. If a state university develops a concept of "service to the community" as its central ideal, as against more remote academic aspirations, this may have its origins in a sense of insecurity, but it will not be innocent in application. To be effective, the projected myth cannot be restricted to holiday speeches or to testimony before legislative committees. It will inevitably color many aspects of university policy, affecting standards of admission, orientations of research, and the scope of the curriculum. The compulsion to embody the myth in practice has a dual source, reflecting inner needs and outer demands. Externally, those who can enforce demands upon the institution will not be content with empty verbal statements. They will expect conformity and the myth itself will provide a powerful lever to that end.

The executive acts out the myth for reasons of self-expression, but also for quite practical administrative reasons. He requires *some* integrating aid to the making of many diverse day-to-day decisions, and the myth helps to fulfill that need. Sharp discrepancies between theory and practice threaten his own authority in the eyes of subordinates; conformity to the myth will lessen "trouble" with outside groups. Not least important, he can hope that the myth will contribute to a unified sense of mission and thereby to the harmony of the whole. If the administrator is primarily dedicated to maintaining a smooth-running machine, and only weakly committed to substantive aims, these advantages will seem particularly appealing.

In the end, however, whatever their source, myths are institution builders. Making the myth effective willy-nilly entrenches particular objectives and capabilities, although these may not be the ones that initially inspired the sponsors of the enterprise. Myth-making may have roots in a sensed need to improve efficiency and morale; but its main office is to help create an integrated social organism.

The art of the creative leader is the art of institution-building, the reworking of human and technological materials to fashion an organism that embodies new and enduring values. The opportunity to do this depends on a considerable sensitivity to the politics of internal change. This is more than a struggle for power among contending groups and leaders. It is equally a matter of avoiding recalcitrance and releasing energies. Thus winning consent to new directions depends on how secure the participants feel. When many routine problems of technical and human organization remain to be solved, when the minimum conditions for holding the organization together are only precariously met, it is difficult to expend energy on long-range planning and even harder to risk experimental programs. When the organization is in good shape from an engineering standpoint it is easier to put ideals into practice. Old activities can be abandoned without excessive strain if, for example, the costs of relatively inefficient but morale-saving transfer and termination can be absorbed. Security is bartered for consent. Since this bargain is seldom sensed as truly urgent, a default of leadership is the more common experience.

On the same theme, security can be granted, thereby releasing energies for creative change, by examining established procedures to distinguish those important to a sense of security from those essential to the aims of the enterprise. Change should focus on the latter; stability can be assured to practices that do not really matter so far as objectives are concerned but which do satisfy the need to be free from threatening change. Many useless industrial conflicts have been fought to protect prerogative and deny security, with but little effect on the ultimate competence of the firm.

If one of the great functions of administration is the exertion of cohesive force in the direction of institutional security, another great function is the creation of conditions that will make possible in the future what is excluded in the present. This requires a strategy of change that looks to the attainment of new capabilities more nearly fulfilling the truly felt needs and aspirations of the institution. The executive becomes a statesman as he makes the transition from administrative management to institutional leadership.

Index

Index

Roles, of organizations, 82–89
  assigned, 91–93
  and competence, 87–88
  and self-conceptions, 84–85
Ruttenberg, H. J., 109

Sears, Roebuck and Co., 54–55
Self-images, and institutionalization, 17–18
Self-maintenance of organizations, and institutionalization, 20–21
Selznick, P., 42, 45, 54, 123
Simon, H. A., 79, 80, 94
Smithburg, D. W., 80, 94
Social composition of organizations
  and critical decision, 57
  and distinctive competence, 46–47
Social structure of administrative organizations, 15–16
  elements of, 91–101
  and historical phases, 102–107
  and precarious values, 119–133
Speier, H., 68, 69, 70
State, Department of, 51–52

Statesmanship, 4–5
  and definition of mission, 70 n.
  and institutional leadership, 37
Stein, H., 13
Stogdill, R. M., 22
Stone, C. P., 102
Strategy, military
  and capability, 11–12, 71–73, 78–79
  and political aims, 75–79
Survival of institutions, and distinctive identity, 63
Sward, K., 110

Taylor, D. W., 102
Technological orientation
  and dispensability of leadership, 74–75
  and political-military strategy, 75–79
  retreat to, 74–82
Tennessee Valley Authority, 42–45
Thompson, V. A., 80, 94
Trade-unions, 21

Ulrich, D. N., 38
Unification of U.S. military agencies, 10–12, 19